# DELUSION AND DREAM

## AND OTHER ESSAYS

DELUSION AND DREAM

AND OTHER ESSAYS

# Delusion and Dream

## AND OTHER ESSAYS

*by*

Sigmund Freud

*edited and with an introduction by Philip Rieff*

BEACON PRESS                     BOSTON

# Note

*Delusion and Dream in Jensen's "Gradiva"* is translated in full for the first time by Harry Zohn, from the second edition of Freud's *Gesammelte Schriften*.

"The Relation of the Poet to Daydreaming," first published in *Neue Revue*, Volume I (1908), was translated by I. F. Grant Duff.

The translation of "The Occurrence in Dreams of Material from Fairy Tales" is by James Strachey, from the text first published in Volume I of the *Internationale Zeitschrift für Psychoanalyse* (1913).

Douglas Bryan translated "A Connection Between a Symbol and a Symptom," which Freud first published in the *Zeitschrift*, Volume IV (1916).

Helen M. Downey translated *Gradiva: A Pompeiian Fancy*, by Wilhelm Jensen.

# *Contents*

# Contents

# Introduction

## I

When, fifty years ago, in the summer of 1906, Freud wrote *Delusion and Dream*, he took, for the first time in detail, a fictional character as his patient. Norbert Hanold's delusions, his dreams, are the deliberate craft of a novelist's mind. The minor German-Danish writer, Wilhelm Jensen, had supplied Freud with a novel, not a case history. To have treated the novel as Freud did, with the aplomb of the case historian, marks a notable advance of his ambition, and contributes as well one of the most readable and instructive essays to the Freudian canon.

For a brief period early in his career, Freud had stopped short, dismayed before the opposition between fact and fiction. Crucial childhood memories that his patients invariably recounted to him turned out to be fictitious. But then he discovered that a seduction need only have been imagined to be true, and this notion of a true fiction saved him from a narrowing dependence on fact. The conventional distinction between matters-of-fact and fantasy—even fantasy organized in the cleverest and most shareable way, as art—dissolved. Thus equipped with an interpretive device that could subdue the entire world of the imagination, Freud undertook several raids into its major settlements, such as the novel, in search of psychological (if not literal) truth.

1

The study of Jensen's *Gradiva,* and the other psychiatric studies of the imagination collected in this volume, reflect Freud's ambition to read the truth back into every fiction. Nothing falls outside the range of the "meaningful and interpretable." Whether the dreams of Norbert Hanold related in *Gradiva* were fictitious or represent repressed knowledge on the part of the novelist, Jensen himself, in no way affects Freud's analysis. "Those dreams which have never been dreamed," Freud wrote, "those created by authors and attributed to fictitious characters in the context of their stories," reveal as much, to the psychoanalytic view, as the dreams of real patients. Of course Freud did try to examine the novelist, Jensen, as well as the novel, *Gradiva.* He sent a number of polite psychoanalytical inquiries, and Jensen replied somewhat testily. We have Freud's hypothetical account of the source of Jensen's inspiration in remarks made before the Vienna Psychoanalytical Society in 1907, the year *Delusion and Dream* was first published. Nevertheless, Freud no more required a case history of Jensen to understand *Gradiva* than he needed to interrogate Norbert Hanold, the novel's hero, in order to dissect his dreams.

Freud did say that no dream could be interpreted without possessing the associations of the patient. But he said as well that associations are unnecessary when one can interpret the dream symbolically; the dream reveals the patient, whatever he may choose to tell about it. So, too, Freud did insist that psychoanalytic interpretation can be properly administered only under the circumstances of therapy. Yet, even while he strikes the attitude of the fastidious therapist, his interpretive method inclines to a gluttonous absorption of all subjects, including those that have not given their consents. Even in the innocent hat, Freud could detect a hidden phallic meaning. (See his essay on "A Connection Between a Symbol and a Symptom," pages 143-144 of this volume.) Given his persuasive capacity for seeing through things to their meanings, Freud found the world of the literary imagination entirely submissive. Jensen might resist. But like a hat or any other prop on the stage of universal meanings, Jensen's leading character was utterly cooperative. Norbert Hanold allows his unconscious to be undressed with the greatest of ease by Zoë, his lost love turned analyst for the finding, and then by Freud, the analyst of lost loves. The fictional character becomes the ideally docile patient of psychoanalysis.

## II

It was Jung who had commended *Gradiva* to Freud. But Freud had no need to catch the fever of Jung's nascent ambition to make psychology the science of practically everything. The aggressive energy, the imperial desire to pacify some unknown province of the mind, was always there. Freud rightly called himself an intellectual *conquistador.* The clinic, however, was not his empire nor the successful treatment of patients his prize. The meticulous collector of clinical data was at the same time a specimen nineteenth-century Moses of theory, leading an intellectual "movement," preaching a rationalist doctrine which was to discipline the rabble of empiricists who had shortened the vision of science. To re-establish the unity of science on the basis of a new rational consciousness, to prescribe practical and ethical as well as speculative goals, was the promise held out in turn by a number of new sciences. Marx had created a master science out of political economy. Comte, then Spencer, asserted sociology. Freud developed the present claim for psychology. These variegated offerings of belief in the form of scientific theory evoke the zealous mood of Freudianism. When once one penetrates the self-advertisement of Freudianism as a thoroughly empirical psychology, it appears as the most influential heir of nineteenth-century scientific rationalism, which advanced so many confident suggestions on how we ought to live. And it is admirably suited to perform its practical role. Better than any other recent science, social or natural, it fulfills the missionary requirements of being both esoteric (read, "scientific") and popular (read, "easily grasped and applied") at the same time.

Earlier Nietzsche had been favorably attracted to psychology as a possible secular guide to the conduct of life. In *Beyond Good and Evil,* aphorism twenty-three, he made the prophecy that Freud confirms:

This immense and almost new domain of dangerous knowledge. . . . Never yet did a *profounder* world of insight reveal itself to daring travellers and adventurers, and the psychologists who thus "make a sacrifice"—it is *not* the *sacrificio dell' intelleto,* on the contrary!— will at least be entitled to demand in return that psychology shall once more be recognized as the Queen of the sciences, for whose service and equipment the other sciences exist. For psychology is once more the path to the fundamental problems.

The fundamental problems to which Nietzsche alludes are entirely personal—even intimate. They are the problems of the psychological man, who in our time has succeeded the economic man as the dominant moral type of Western culture. History again has produced a type specially able to endure it—in this period, the trained egoist, the private man.

From the arenas of public failure, the psychological man turns inward to the re-examination of himself and his personal affections. For this massive internalizing of interest by Western man, a new secular pietism was needed. Freudian psychology, with its ingenious interpretations of the inner life and of immediate familial experience as its key, exactly fits this need.

Fettered to no routine of confirmation more reliable than the belief of its adherents and patients, Freud's doctrine lives as a sturdy and successful Roman among the effete and scrupulous Greeks of scientific psychology. The psychology of William James, for example, presented no challenge to Freud. Unsympathetic, uninterested in whatever threatened to narrow his own vast theoretical ambition, Freud dismissed the Jamesian psychology without argument.[1] But because he never took his competitors very seriously or deferred to a regimen of scientific detachment, we have the great quasi-ethical works of Freud, masked as empirical psychology, that we should not otherwise have had. Seventeen years after Freud's death it is possible to see clearly the ambivalent nature of his genius. As an empirical worker, he looked not for evidence but for meaning. As a rationalist theoretician, he looked for evidence first, to certify what he took to be a universal grammar of psychological meanings. The two sides of his mind—the empiricist and the rationalist—never examined each other. Indeed, they were almost unaware of each other's separate existences. For this reason, and from the earliest stage of his thought, Freud could blandly assume the identity of psychoanalysis as a

[1] Freud, *General Introduction to Psychoanalysis* (New York, 1943), p. 344.

therapy (empirical) and as a theory (rational). Nevertheless, in the undeclared war between the empiricist and the
rationalist within Freud's mind, the rationalist easily won
out. Meaning was prior to event, not something to be constructed after the event. Neurosis itself was identified as the
failure of the individual to understand the meanings which
preside over his own behavior. Not that rational understanding as such can annul a neurosis. Norbert Hanold is far from
cured when Zoë, his analyst, helps him to work through his
delusions to a proto-Freudian understanding of them. Freud,
the therapist, does not claim that his ideas alone could cure.
Cure is a fact that can emerge only through the long pro-
bation of experience. But as the master of a theory that must
be accepted as a personal guide to life in order to be understood, Freud declares that his analysis of the emotions is itself
positively therapeutic. To this extent, throughout his work,
Freud tends to underestimate the recalcitrance of fact, its
capacity to escape the design of meaning any interpreter
can lay down around it.

### III

To a psychology whose singular capacity is the liquidation of each small fact into its larger meaning, literature was
a ready-made source book of meanings. At least from 1898
onward Freud had been reading novels as if they were
symptoms, in search of confirmation for his theories. In letters to his confidant of those inventive years, Wilhelm
Fliess, Freud briefly dissected two stories by C. F. Meyer,
*Die Richterin* and *Die Hochzeit des Mönchs.* Already in
this dissection a number of procedures standard to the
Freudian psychiatry appear in use—particularly the trans-

fer of present motives into past, which Freud applied as an exorcist to neurotics but as an encomiast to artists. For in particular among these two nervous types, present experience repeats the past, in some more or less transparent disguise. Referring at once to the author and to his fictions, Freud remarks to Fliess "how in the process of fantasy formation in later years the imagination seizes on a new experience and projects it into the past." It is this endowment of the past with life, through the agency of the imagination, that characterizes both the artist and the neurotic. Thus Freud first used fiction to "illustrate magnificently" the psychological process. However, the present essay, *Delusion and Dream*, marks the one occasion where Freud systematically treated an entire piece of fiction, transforming *Gradiva*, by means of his voracious interpretive method, from an anticipation of psychoanalytic truth into an illustration of it.

To use a novel as an illustration of scientific doctrine is not an altogether proper thing for a good positivist to do, and Freud had his qualms over the scientific legitimacy of his subject. Rather ruefully he remarks, in the early *Studies in Hysteria*, that his case histories "read like novels." It is as if the erratic maladies of his patients were, from his point of view, a vaguely illicit subject better left to the novelist. True, as a scientist, he could declare himself grandly on the side of art. In *Delusion and Dream* and elsewhere, he "dared, against the protests of orthodox science, to take sides with the ancients and the superstitious." Great art like *Oedipus Rex* and *Hamlet*, minor works like *Gradiva*— the entire inventory of world culture seemed to serve, however unawares, the psychoanalytic truth. Yet set against even his strictest caveats on the condensed and primly logical operations of "orthodox science," Freud's declared preferences for art nevertheless leave it the inferior precursor of science. The testimony he has art give is not for itself but in praise of his own insight. Myth, fairy tale, the novel, poetry— all art was suddenly enriched. What remained, in order to exploit these hidden resources, was to refine a work of art until its pure meanings had been extracted.

All behavior, not just works of art, invites this refining process. Any act can be symptomatic—the rage of a psychotic, a senseless compulsion, a dream ("our normal psychosis"), a trivial error or slip of the tongue. Even as Freud exposes the work of art as little more than an elaborate symptomatic appeal, in a compensatory fashion he dignifies the trivial acts and objects of ordinary psychic life to something meaningful in almost the literary sense. At times Freud's results verge on the grotesque, as in the present essay on the connection between a symbol and a symptom. Here we see most clearly how the Freudian science may give itself over to a kind of literary extravagance, to the discovery through plastic analogues of improbable symbolic equivalences among objects and actions.

It is appropriate that psychoanalysis assume some of the prerogatives of an aesthetics. For in the Freudian view man is an aesthetic animal, and his symptoms may be comprehended as the artfulness of his will. Penetrated by psychoanalysis, everyday life takes on the appearance of a backstage cluttered with old scenery, every piece symbolic of something. The trained human actor picks his way through life, aware of the strange plots all this detritus still might serve. Untrained, we are nevertheless very artful, engaged

in a continuous act of deception first of all before the naive
audience of our own consciousness. Freud would have
agreed with Emerson that we are greatly more poetic than
we know—"poets in our drudgery, poets in our eyes, and
ears, and skin." The psychoanalytic view transforms all men
into poets—incurable symbolists, telling unknown secrets
with every word, memorializing them in every institution.
By installing in each of us—not just in a privileged class of
the talented—a psychic agency for dramatizing motives,
Freud democratized art. Art becomes, in his view, a public
companion to the dream. Equally, the dream becomes an
inward artistry lacking the power to communicate[2] until

[2] Of course, Freud had his forerunners in this conjecture. For one of
the few pre-Freudian contributions to the explanation of dreams which
still stands up under the weight and detail of the Freudian inferences, see
the essay by Frances Power Cobbe, "Dreams as Illustrations of Unconscious
Cerebration," in her *Darwinism in Morals and Other Essays* (London,
1872), and especially this passage (pp. 337-338): "We have been accustomed to consider the myth-creating power of the human mind as one
specially belonging to the earlier stages of growth of society and of the
individual. [But] this instinct exists in every one of us, and exerts itself
with more or less energy through the whole of our lives. In hours of waking
consciousness, indeed, it is suppressed, or has only the narrowest range of
exercise." But the daytime "play of the myth-making faculty is nothing
compared to its achievements during sleep. . . . At the very least half our
dreams (unless I greatly err) are nothing else than myths formed by
unconscious cerebration on the same approved principles, whereby Greece
and India and Scandinavia gave to us the stories which we were once
pleased to set apart as 'mythology' proper. Have we not here, then, evidence
that there is a real law of the human mind causing us constantly to com-
pose ingenious fables explanatory of the phenomena around us,—a law
which only sinks into abeyance in the waking hours of persons in whom
the reason has been highly cultivated, but which resumes its sway even
over their well-tutored brains when they sleep?" It is, I think, a remarkable
passage, documenting the early confluence between a rising science of
mythology and a rising new psychology. Miss Cobbe was one of that
company of first-rate minds, now forgotten, who wrote for the great
quarterly journals of nineteenth-century England and kept at least their
section of the public superbly well educated.

Otto Rank, in various supplements to Freud's *Interpretation of Dreams*
(see "Traum und Dichtung," "Traum und Mythus") and in *Der Künstler,*

released into the public domain by the Freudian method. Although the extension of educated interest beyond the poetry and art of professionals to that of children, primitives, and the insane—art latent in everybody—antedates Freud's writings, it is mainly under the impact of Freudian ideas that art has become, next to dreams, the acknowledged *via regia* into the depths. Art has been even more fully exploited by Jung and his followers, who take works of the literary and religious imagination as their chief psychological documents.

Freud's tendency to normalize art, his notion that we are all artists informally—in the dream, the symptomatic act—should be balanced against his better-known inclination to retract art into neurosis. Psychoanalysis inherits a good deal of that hostility to art which accompanied the positivist attitude. The artist was considered vocationally susceptible to special weaknesses of character; what the artist does was thought itself to be "regressive," "childish," "escapist." (This is a leading theme of "The Relation of the Poet to Daydreaming," pages 122-133 of the present volume.) Scientists, too, may suffer from the weaknesses that poetry repairs; they only mend themselves differently. Norbert Hanold, as Freud interprets him, is part scientist, part artist. He has both intellectual capacity and imagination. But because he suffers from a "separation of imagination and intellectual capacity," he is "destined to be a poet or neurotic." Being an archaeologist, and therefore having science to put in the service of his imagination, Norbert develops an elaborate

---

draws attention to passages in Wagner's *Meistersinger*, in Schopenhauer and Kant, which suggest this intimate relation of the dream with poetry and myth.

delusion about a Pompeiian girl in order to meet again the girl who lives next door. Only a neurotic—or a poet—could become so opaque about his erotic desires.

For the work of art as such, for its conventions and history, Freud cared very little. Not unexpectedly, he sometimes badly misconstrued a work in his eagerness to use it illustratively. As an exegete, Freud is often merely tendentious. (See his essay on "The Moses of Michelangelo.") As a commentator, he made some large and naive mistakes. (See his little book on Leonardo da Vinci, written a year after the essay on *Gradiva*.) But once we have understood that to Freud the criticism of art promised more than the practice of it, we can no longer fairly read his aesthetic commentary against particular works with an eye toward its accuracy of assessment. The work of art is something to see through; it is presumably best explained by something other than—even contradicting—itself. Every work of art is to Freud simply a museum piece of the unconscious, a chance to contemplate the unconscious frozen into one of its possible gestures.

To be sure, Freud does not merely dismiss the artist after seeing through his art; neither does he merely psychoanalyze him. The artist is gifted in a rare manner for which Freud demands respect and attention. Lacking the kind of knowledge scientists and men of affairs use, nevertheless the artist has something better: "psychic knowledge." Being endowed in a way superior to the ordinary neurotic with certain atavistic capacities, the artist can "draw from sources that have not yet been made accessible to science." It was indeed the function of psychoanalysis to penetrate the atavistic capacity, to bring it into the orbit of science. But what will happen to the artist when the sources of his inspiration are opened up for study and scientific exploitation? Rilke, for one, when importuned by Lou Andreas-Salome, a friend he shared with Freud, declined analysis, for fear it might sap his creative powers. And probably he was right. Freud does not say straight out, but he implies, that science, as it is successful, renders art less necessary. The great rationalist slogan of psychoanalysis—*where id is, there let ego be*— implicitly offers science as the successor not only of religion but of its original handmaiden, art. So far as he takes Freud's rationalist psychology seriously, every artist must face Rilke's option: whether through psychoanalysis he wishes to return to a grammar school of science, in order to learn the sub-artistic meanings of his personal language.

IV

Psychoanalysis, as a science of the emotions, must always proceed by indirection. For the Freudian psychology contends that the emotions are prevented, not only by the weight of authority represented in the culture but by a self-canceling relation among the emotions themselves, from being expressed directly. Therefore our inner lives are not simply or directly embodied in actions, but become expressive, "symbolic," as the emotions are given distorted and partial discharge. Literature is merely the craft some personalities develop at exhibiting their deeper emotions. In a more cohesive society, the exhibition may take place within the added safety of collective fantasy: religion, myth, superstition. When social enforcements have become frayed— when, in Kafka's memorable phrase, all religions have dissolved into sects of one—this same drive toward expressiveness takes the form of outright neurosis. The shared expressions fragment into private aberration, becoming subject to the same sort of analysis that Freud imposed on symptomatic actions. Thus art, as well as religion, is transformed into varieties of emotive statement.

Of course Freud recognized that the emotive statements of art and neurosis differ fundamentally. A work of art is a system of shareable meanings, as a dream or daydream is not; a dream is merely expressive, not art but artistic, while the daydream is usually of no interest to others. In his essay on the relation between the poet and daydreaming, Freud distinguishes stages of private emotional expressiveness with respect to communicative intent, climaxing in art. In the jargon of the "ego psychology" wing of Freudian orthodoxy (I quote from Ernst Kris, a leading intelligence of this school), the artist during creation is, like the neurotic, subject to "ego regression." But, in contrast to the neurotic,

. . . it is a partial and temporary ego regression, one controlled by the ego which retains the function of establishing contact with an audience. The artist identifies himself with his public in order to invite their participation, a participation postulating their subsequent identification with him. No such identification prevails in the patient; his speech is basically soliloquy.

The step from soliloquy to public address is therefore the step from neurosis to art. The artist, unlike the neurotic, has succeeded in inviting an audience to share his emotional prepossessions with him. Only if the neurotic can evoke credence and emotional response in others does he become in this general sense an artist—or perhaps a religious virtuoso. Surely this makes a difference, and Freud acknowledges it. But the difference is not as great as may appear. Freud continues to assume that the artist, however trimmed and acceptable the public utterance with which he ends, begins at the exact same point as the neurotic. It thus becomes legitimate for the analytic interpreter to cancel the intellectual or publicly shareable meanings which distinguish a novel or poem from neurotic fantasy or dream; he may go about the routine transposition of public statement back into private intention. Indeed, the successful patient, who makes an identification with a representative public of one, the analyst, himself becomes something of an artist. His art is also a form of catering to his public; he invites it to participate in his own emotional life.

Of creativity as an intellectual process Freud intimates almost nothing. He can conceive of art only in the romantic sense, as evocative of an emotional response through the identification of the artist and his public, not as a matrix for detached and thoughtful interest. Literary works supply, along with religion, significant data for Freud's moral science—data to be cross-sectioned so as to get at those stratified deposits of aggressive energy and unsocial wish from which moralities grow. But in Freud's opinion the artist, like the religious man, has no critical aptitude. No more than religion is art a final resource of judgment; it merely detours into expression what must be recovered in rational understanding.

What is characteristic in Freudian analysis is just this enterprise of recovery: beginning with the reduction of behavior to emotive statement and proceeding through a more or less set sequence of ingeniously rational interpretations. As Freud says of the dream, it is "only a substitute for a rational process of thought"; it can always be "interpreted— that is to say, translated into a rational process." From its eighteenth-century beginnings in the study of comparative religion, when a universal substrate of natural belief was uncovered beneath all creedal varieties, through the positivist period in the middle of the last century, when the mythic and metaphysical were reduced to forerunners of the scientific attitude, to the psychological age in which we now live, the main effort of the modern intelligence has been to rationalize not only the production of goods but also our literary and imaginative productions. In this tradition, the scientific effort characteristically treats works of the imagination as, so to speak, a primitive level of truth—which, taken by itself, is false.

All the terms—"distortion," "projection," "displacement," "condensation"—which Freud uses in interpreting psychological artifacts such as dreams, errors, art, myth, refer to this double level of truth. It is significant that Freud characteristically speaks of dreaming as "work." What the imagination does, in his view, is indeed work; it works to distort, complicate, individualize, and thereby conceal the potent, sub-individual wishes and desires. Exactly the same mechanisms prevail in the special kind of symptomatic statement which is art. There is the gross platitude of motive, and the individual level at which motive is embedded in the symptom. The narrow selection of universal motives exhibited by psychoanalysis leaves little for the artist to do, in Freud's view, except specify them. From being creative, the artist becomes, newly understood, "recreative." The highest task of psychoanalytic interpretation is to work back through expressive statements to the repressed motive thus hidden especially from its carrier. Art, by Freudian definition, is not only a mode of fulfilling tabooed wishes, of enacting them in fantasy. The perhaps superior work of the imagination is self-concealment, to keep us at a safe distance from ourselves and from each other. For its power, art depends upon an appeal that is hidden from the artist as well as the audience. Freud can take it for granted that Jensen could not have understood what he was saying in *Gradiva;* otherwise, the whole appeal of the novel, first to himself and then to his audience, would have been dissipated.

It follows from the essential dualism of Freud's interpretive scheme—between "manifest" and "latent" contents —that the task of interpretation enlarges considerably. Given the manifest level upon which art proceeds, the task of analytically reducing art to its latent meanings will become all the more important. The act of criticism gets built into the creative effort itself, for the secondary or manifest order of truth must always be interpreted—that is, processed back to its universal symbolic meanings. Freud assumed that one can understand the emotions only through their symptomatic paraphrase. Further, he assumed that psychic expressions are never directly intelligible, even when they appear to be so, but conceal meanings and motives that have to be dug out. Once either of these assumptions is made, critical interpretation becomes not a supplementary but an integral and even commanding feature in the work of the imagination. Take Freud's model instance of the work of the imagination, dreams. Given "the usual ambiguity of dreams, as of all other psychopathological formations," each dream becomes susceptible to more than one interpretation. Interpretation, Freud concludes, is necessary in order to complete the dream; indeed, some "over-interpretation" is always necessary. The present efflorescence of literary criticism—which surely has been influenced by the psychoanalytic style of interpretation—follows closely this model relation of neurotic symptom and medicinal interpretation. Works of art are characteristically esteemed for their "ambiguity," or richness of texture; and some of our great modern pieces of fiction, as if inviting the completion of an interpretation, seem deliberately unfinished (*vide* the novels of Kafka) or are themselves constructed as many-layered conundrums, soliciting (as James Joyce said of his own works) a lifetime of interpretive meditation to decipher them.

Yet at the same time that Freudianism enormously increases the ambit and necessity of interpretation, its implications are reductive. Nothing more clearly overrides the autonomy of the aesthetic imagination than Freud's attempt to rationalize it. As an intellectual equivalent of the industrial process, rationalist science finds a uniform production of symbol and myths and works of the imagination so that all these can be classified and identified with each other. As the early Deist and rationalist students of comparative religion simplified Christian dogma until they discovered in it the same ultimate truths as, say, in Zoroastrianism, so the modern psychological rationalist simplifies the variety of emotive expression to find the same meanings beneath. The separate and often irreconcilable detail of myths, religions, dreams, and art are made, under psychoanalytic heat, to melt and merge. The Freudian method is thus entirely reductionist as to genre. It tends to reduce art, myth, dream, fairy tale alike to the same basic stock of plots and symbols. For psychology is the science of motivation, and motive-wise different works of art may look very similar. An interest in

motives shared by the generality of men offers little basis
upon which to distinguish among works of the imagination.
(Hence the significance of Freud's examining the occurrence
in dreams of material from fairy tales, pages 134-142 of the
present volume.) Further, this exclusively motivational analysis retains no way of dealing with what aestheticians call
the sensuous surface of a work of art. The qualitative experience of the senses is dismissed by Freud as mere "fore-
pleasure"; his aesthetic criticism is purely intellectual.

What Freud has to say about art applies to all art, good
and bad. It is somewhat accidental to the psychoanalytically
minded critic what is being scrutinized. In various writings, when he turns, for illustrations of psychological
dilemmas, to *Oedipus* and *Hamlet*, to *Macbeth*, to *Richard
III*, to plays of Ibsen, Freud develops some brilliant insights.
Yet it all seems very arbitrary. Works of lesser stature could
as well have exemplified his theme. It is revealing that
Freud's one full-scale examination of a novel—the present
*Delusion and Dream*—fixes on a work of fragile aesthetic
merit. But aesthetic merit, or the limit of a particular genre,
is not Freud's concern. His interest caught on *Gradiva* not
for any reason of literary excellence, but ostensibly because
the novel could be read as an ingenious prevision of the
psychoanalytic love cure. We may agree, I think, that *Gradiva* would not be very memorable in itself, lacking Freud's
gloss—and this perhaps is an ideal state of affairs, from the
view of psychoanalytic interpretive technique.

v

I should not like to imply that *Gradiva* supplied the
raw material of Freud's reductive technique, and no more.

However slight a work, *Gradiva* is to some extent true to the center of the novelistic tradition. It relates a quest for the recovery of the personal self; it is a story that praises the liquidation of the burden of the past and ends happily, with the opposite sexes walking into an open future. Just these are the themes most central to the novel since the inception of the romantic period of our culture. And since depth psychology, too—as well as the novel—lives off the presuppositions and questions of the romantic period, it seems apt that Freud acknowledged what happens in the novel as an analogue to the healing mission of his own science.

This raises a larger question, which can only be touched on here: the question of the relation between psychology and the novel. Certainly at the present time it would seem to be a congenial relation. Like the novel, Freudian psychology still accepts the individual as the unit of analysis. Yet, in historical context, the general habits of introspection and solicitude toward the self which Freud's method sponsors raise at best a defensive enclave into which the individual may retreat. The literature and science of the individual— the novel and depth psychology—take on the added import of consolation, in an age in which the individual counts for less and less. For in our society the individual has been severely challenged. Change has been built into the ordinary rhythms of social life. Caught up in the frightening acceleration of historical events, personal decision has lost the moral import it had in slower times. As if in compensation, just when he is becoming a cipher, the modern individual has learned to play with utter earnestness at the ancient problem of "discovering himself." Psychotherapy cannot be for most more than a luxury experience, a bracketed area in which the individual can face the problem of making decisions, as if they are his to make.

Nevertheless, it is fair to say also that depth psychology repudiates the conception of the moral life which is implied in the novel. Against the novelistic tradition, which is Protestant and individual, our psychology has emphasized that the self is a fiction—a composite of instinctual and social mandates. In his psychological theory, Freud allows only the smallest margin for the self-determining individual. And this self-determination (located in the *ego*) amounts merely to a skill at playing off against one another the massive subindividual (*id*) and supra-individual (*super-ego*) forces by which the self is shaped. Idiosyncrasy, decision, habits of moral stocktaking can be referred back to the generic motives which they merely exemplify. And not only in theory but in the presumptive rules of interpretation which are set down in therapy, there is a rebuke to our inherited sense of self. To be always plucking universal motifs from behind the ear of the prone subject, to seize exemplifications of sexual symbols out of a hat—surely this magic is impressive but more impressive is its ethical import.

In his essay on Jensen's *Gradiva*, Freud wears the face of an emancipator, physician to sick individuality in search of its abrogation in the instinctual life. Norbert Hanold, as Freud tells us, suffers alienation from love. His illness is essentially "the rejection of eroticism." But sick as his erotic nature is, much as it has disordered his reason, he is still driven, by the very agency of his delusion, within reach of a lover. And love, incarnate in the long-lost Zoë, cures him. According to the erotic ethic of Freudianism, he has been saved; his body has been reconciled with his mind. The lesson of Norbert Hanold's life, that one cannot starve the emotions, that one has to obey the imperatives of nature, Freud takes as the model psychoanalytic remedy.

Yet Freud had another face—turned always against "the lie of salvation" [3] in any form, including salvation through sexuality. The erotic ethic of *Delusion and Dream* is only part of the Freudian ethics, perhaps the lesser part. Freud is not only the approving commentator on Zoë's maneuvers toward the act of love. So far as he encouraged the passions, he did so in a complex and self-canceling way. *Delusion and Dream*, and the essays included in this volume, give little idea of the reflective discipline of self-consciousness which he made a prerequisite for divesting oneself of one's symptoms, if not one's deeper illness. If, in *Delusion and Dream*, Freud is the champion of the erotic life, he is also, in other places, the master of an ironic view of life. It is a fairly chilly permissiveness that psychoanalysis fosters— more a matter of prudence than passion, more science than sex. While psychoanalysis is engaged in permitting us to experience our emotions without hindrance from images of the past, it also engages its adherents in a more dispassionate task: that of testing the logic of the emotions themselves.

PHILIP RIEFF

*Brandeis University*

[3] See his letters to Wilhelm Fliess in *The Origins of Psychoanalysis* (New York, 1954), p. 366.

# DELUSION AND DREAM

## AND OTHER ESSAYS

# DELUSION AND DREAM

## AND OTHER ESSAYS

# Delusion and Dream

In a circle of men who take it for granted that the basic riddle of the dream has been solved by the efforts of the present writer,[1] curiosity was aroused one day concerning those dreams which have never been dreamed, those created by authors and attributed to fictitious characters in the context of their stories. The proposal to submit this kind of dream to investigation might appear idle and strange; but from one point of view it could be considered justifiable. For it is by no means generally believed that the dreamer dreams something meaningful and interpretable. Science and the majority of educated people smile when one offers them the task of interpreting dreams. Only the common man who still clings to superstition, thereby giving continuity to the convictions of the ancients, will not refrain from interpreting dreams, and the writer of *The Interpretation of Dreams* has dared, against the protests of orthodox science, to take sides with the ancients and the superstitious. He is, of course, far from accepting in dreams a prevision of the future, for the disclosure of which man has ever striven by illicit means and in vain. He could not, however, completely reject the connections of dreams with the future, for, after completing some arduous analysis, the dreams seemed to him to represent *the fulfillment of a wish* of the dreamer;

[1] See *The Interpretation of Dreams* (1900), translated by James Strachey, in *Complete Psychological Works of Sigmund Freud*, Standard Edition, Vols. IV and V (London, 1953).

and who could dispute that wishes are preponderantly concerned with the future?

I have just said that a dream is a fulfilled wish. Whoever is not afraid to toil through a difficult book, whoever does not demand that a complicated problem be insincerely and untruthfully presented to him as easy and simple, to save his own effort, may seek in the above-mentioned *Interpretation of Dreams* ample proof of this statement and may, until then, cast aside the objection that will surely be expressed against the equating of dreams with wish-fulfillment.

We have, however, anticipated quite a bit. The question is not now one of establishing whether the meaning of a dream is, in every case, to be stated as the fulfillment of a wish, or, just as frequently, as an anxious expectation, an intention or deliberation, and so on. The first question is, rather, whether a dream has any meaning at all, whether one should grant it the value of a psychic process. Science answers "no"; it explains the dream as a purely physiological process, behind which one need not seek meaning, significance, or intention. Physical stimuli play, during sleep, on the psychic instrument and bring into consciousness at different times various ideas devoid of psychic coherence. Dreams are comparable only to convulsions, not to movements of the psychic life.

In this dispute over the evaluation of dreams, creative writers seem to be on the side of the ancients, superstitious people, and the author of *The Interpretation of Dreams*. For, when they cause the people created by their imagination to dream, they follow the everyday experience that people's thoughts and feelings continue into sleep, and they seek only to depict the psychic states of their heroes through the dreams of the latter. Storytellers are valuable allies, and their testimony is to be rated high, for they usually know many things between heaven and earth that are not yet dreamt of in our philosophy. In psychological insights, indeed, they are far ahead of us ordinary people, because they draw from sources that have not yet been made accessible to science. If this partisanship of creative writers for the meaningful nature of dreams were only more unequivocal! Very sharp criticism might object that writers take sides neither for nor against the psychic significance of an isolated dream; they are satisfied to show how the sleeping psyche stirs under the stimuli which have remained active in it as offshoots of waking life.

However, our interest in the way in which storytellers make use of dreams is not made less intense by this sobering thought. Even if our investigation should teach us nothing new about the nature of dreams, it may perhaps afford us, from this angle, some insight into the nature of the creative literary process. If actual dreams are considered to be unrestrained and irregular phenomena, what about the free re-creations of such dreams? But there is much less freedom and arbitrariness in psychic life than we are inclined to believe, perhaps none at all. What is called chance by the outside world resolves itself, as we know, into laws; also, what we call arbitrariness in psychic life is based on laws that are at present but dimly surmised. Let us, then, take a close look.

There are two possible methods for this investigation; one is the delving into a special case, the dream-creations of one writer in one of his works; the other consists in bringing together and comparing all the examples of the use of dreams which are found in the works of different story-tellers. The second way seems to be by far the more effective, perhaps the only justifiable one, for it frees us immediately from the dangers inherent in the artificial concept of "the writer" as a unity. This unity falls to pieces in investigations of widely different writers, some of whom we are wont to admire, individually, as the most profound connoisseurs of psychic life. Yet these pages will be devoted to an investigation of the former kind. It so happened, in the group of men who started the idea, that someone remembered that the piece of fiction he had most recently enjoyed contained several dreams which looked at him with familiar expression, as it were, and invited him to try with them the method of *The Interpretation of Dreams.* He admitted that the material and setting of the little tale had probably been largely responsible for his enjoyment of it, for the story was unfolded in Pompeii and concerned a young archaeologist who had given up interest in life for that in the remains of the classic past, and now, by a peculiar but absolutely correct detour, was brought back to life. During the perusal of this really poetic material, the reader experienced all sorts of feelings of familiarity and concurrence. The tale was Wilhelm Jensen's *Gradiva,* a little romance designated by its author himself "A Pompeiian Fancy."

In order that my further references may be to familiar material, I must now ask my readers to lay aside this essay and replace it for some time with *Gradiva,* which was published in 1903. To those who have already read *Gradiva* I will recall the content of the story in a short summary and

hope that their memory will of itself restore all the charm
of which the story is thereby divested.

A young archaeologist, Norbert Hanold, has discovered in
Rome, in a collection of antiques, a bas-relief which attracts
him so exceptionally that he is delighted to be able to get an
excellent plaster cast of it which he can hang up in his study
in a German university town and study with interest. The
relief represents a fully developed young girl walking. She
has gathered up her voluminous gown slightly, so that her
sandaled feet become visible. One foot rests wholly on the
ground; the other is raised to follow and touches the ground
only with the tips of the toes, while sole and heel rise almost
perpendicularly. The unusual and especially charming gait
represented had probably aroused the artist's attention, and
now, after so many centuries, captivates the eye of our
archaeological observer.

This interest of the hero in the bas-relief described above
is the basic psychological fact of our story. It is not immediately explicable. "Dr. Norbert Hanold, docent of archaeology, really found in the relief nothing noteworthy for his
science. . . . he could not explain what quality in it had
aroused his attention. He knew only that he had been attracted by something, and this effect of the first view had
remained unchanged since then"; but his imagination does
not cease to be occupied with the relief. He finds in it a
"sense of present time," as if the artist had fixed the picture on the street "from life." He confers a name, Gradiva,
"the girl splendid in walking," upon the girl thus represented, spins a yarn that she is surely the daughter of a
distinguished family, perhaps of a "patrician aedile, whose

office was connected with the worship of Ceres," and is on her way to the temple of the goddess. Then it is repulsive to him to place her calm, serene manner in the hustle and bustle of a metropolis. Rather, he convinces himself that she is to be transported to Pompeii and is walking there somewhere on the peculiar steppingstones which have been excavated; these made a dry crossing possible in rainy weather and yet also afforded passage for chariot-wheels. The cut of her features seems to him Greek, her Hellenic ancestry unquestionable. His entire knowledge of antiquity gradually puts itself at the service of this or other fantasies connected with the relief.

Then, however, a supposedly scholarly problem obtrudes itself upon him and demands to be solved. It is a matter of his passing a critical judgment on "whether the artist had reproduced Gradiva's manner of walking from life." He cannot produce it in himself; in the search for the "real existence" of this gait, he arrives only at "observation from life for the purpose of enlightenment on the matter." This, to be sure, forces him to a mode of action utterly alien to him. "Women had formerly been for him only a conception in marble or bronze, and he had never given his female contemporaries the least consideration." Social life has always seemed an unavoidable torture to him; young ladies whom he meets, in such connections, he fails to see and hear to such a degree that, on the next encounter, he passes them without greeting—which, of course, serves to place him in an unfavorable light with them. Now, however, the scientific task which he has set himself forces him to observe diligently the feet of ladies and girls on the street in dry weather, but especially in wet weather—an activity which nets him many a displeased and many an encouraging glance from those observed. "Yet one was as incomprehensible to him as the other." As a result of these careful studies, he finds that Gradiva's gait cannot be proved really to exist, a fact that fills him with regret and annoyance.

Soon afterwards he has a frightening dream which transports him to old Pompeii on the day of the eruption of Vesuvius and makes him an eyewitness of the destruction of the city. "As he stood thus at the edge of the Forum near the Jupiter temple, he suddenly saw Gradiva a short distance in front of him. Until then no thought of her presence there had moved him, but now suddenly it seemed natural to him, as she was, of course, a Pompeiian girl, that she was living in her native city and, *without his having any suspicion of it, was his contemporary.*" Fear about her impending fate draws from him a cry of warning, in answer to which the unperturbed apparition turns her face toward him. Unconcerned, she continues on her way to the portico of the temple, sits down there on a step and slowly rests her head upon it, while her face keeps growing paler, as if it were turning to white marble. As he hastens after her, he finds her stretched out on the broad step with a calm countenance, as if sleeping; soon the rain of ashes buries her form.

When he awakes, he thinks he is still hearing the confused cries of the Pompeiians, who are seeking safety, and the dully resounding boom of the turbulent sea; but even after his returning senses have recognized these noises as the waking expressions of life in the noisy metropolis, he retains for a long time the belief in the reality of what he has dreamed; when he has finally rid himself of the idea that he was really present, nearly two thousand years ago, at the destruction of Pompeii, there yet remains in him, as a firm conviction, the idea that Gradiva lived in Pompeii and was buried there in the year 79. His fantasies about Gradiva, due to the aftereffects of this dream, continue so that he only now begins to mourn her as lost.

While he leans from his window, preoccupied with these ideas, his attention is attracted by a canary warbling his song in a cage at an open window of the house opposite. Suddenly something like a thrill passes through the man who seems not yet completely awakened from his dream. He believes that he has seen, in the street, a figure like that of his Gradiva and even recognized the gait characteristic of her. Without deliberating he hastens to the street to overtake her, and only the laughter and jeers of the people at his unsuitable morning attire drive him quickly back home. In his room, it is again the singing canary in the cage which occupies him and stimulates him to a comparison with himself. He, too, is sitting in a cage, he finds; yet it is easier for him to leave his cage. As if from an added aftereffect of the dream, perhaps also under the influence of the mild spring air, he decides to take a spring trip to Italy, for which a scientific motive is soon found, even if "the impulse for travel had originated in a nameless feeling."

We will stop a moment at this most loosely motivated journey and take a closer look at the personality as well as the activities of our hero. He still seems to us incomprehensible and foolish; we have no idea of how his special folly is to acquire enough human appeal to compel our interest. It is the privilege of the author of *Gradiva* to leave us in such a quandary; with his beauty of diction and his judicious selection of incident he rewards, for the time being, our confidence and the as yet undeserved sympathy which we are ready to grant to his hero. Of the latter we learn that he is already destined by family tradition to be an antiquarian, has later, in isolation and independence, submerged himself completely in his science, and has withdrawn entirely from life and its pleasures. Marble and bronze are, for his feelings, the only things really alive and expressive of the purpose and value of human life. Yet, perhaps with kind intent, nature has put into his blood a thoroughly unscientific sort of corrective, a most lively imagination, which is able to find expression not only in his dreams, but also in his waking life. By such a separation of imagination and intellectual capacity he is destined to be a poet or a neurotic, and he belongs to that race of beings whose realm is not of this world. So it happens that his interest is fixed upon a bas-relief which represents a girl walking in an unusual manner, that he spins a web of fantasies about her, invents a name and an ancestry for her, and transports the person created by him to Pompeii, which was buried more than eighteen hundred years ago. Finally, after a strange anxiety-dream, he intensifies the fantasy of the existence and destruction of the girl named Gradiva into a delusion which comes to influence his acts. These performances of imagination would appear strange and inscrutable to us if we encountered them in a really living person. Since our hero, Norbert Hanold, is a creature of a writer, we should like to ask the latter timidly if his fancy has been determined by any power other than its own arbitrariness.

We left our hero just as he is apparently being moved by the song of a canary to take a trip to Italy, the motive for which does not seem to be clear to him. We learn, further, that neither destination nor purpose is firmly established in his mind. An inner restlessness and dissatisfaction drive him from Rome to Naples and farther on from there; he gets into the swarm of honeymooners, and, forced to notice the amorous "Augustuses" and "Gretchens," is utterly unable to understand the doings of these couples. He arrives at the conclusion that, of all the follies of mankind, "marriage, at any rate, took the prize as the greatest and most incomprehensible one, and the senseless wedding trips to Italy somehow capped the climax of this buffoonery." At Rome, disturbed in his sleep by the proximity of a loving couple, he flees forthwith to Naples, only to find there another "Augustus" and "Gretchen." As he believes that he gathers from their conversation that the majority of those bird-couples do not intend to nest in the rubble of Pompeii, but to wing their way to Capri, he decides to do what they do not do, and finds himself in Pompeii, "contrary to expectations and intentions," a few days after the beginning of his journey —without, however, finding there the peace he seeks.

The role which, until then, has been played by the honeymoon couples, who made him uneasy and irritated his nerves, is now assumed by houseflies, in which he is inclined to see the incarnation of absolute evil and worthlessness. The two tormentors blend into one; many fly-couples remind him of honeymoon travelers, probably addressing each other, in their language, also as "My only Augustus" and "My sweet Gretchen."

Finally he cannot help admitting "that his dissatisfaction was probably not caused by his surroundings alone, but to a degree had its origin in him." He feels that he is out of sorts because he lacks something without being able to explain what.

The next morning he goes through the *ingresso* to Pompeii and, after taking leave of the guide, roams aimlessly through the city—strangely enough, however, without remembering that he has been present in a dream some time before at the destruction of Pompeii. In the "hot, holy" noon hour which the ancients considered the ghost hour, when the other visitors have taken flight and the heap of ruins, desolate and steeped in sunlight, lies before him, there stirs in him the ability to transport himself back into the buried life, but not with the aid of science. "What it taught was a lifeless, archaeological view, and what came from its mouth was a dead, philological language. These helped in no way to a comprehension with soul, mind, and heart, or whatever one wanted to call it; instead, anyone who harbored a desire for such a comprehension had to stand here alone, among the remains of the past, the only living person in the hot noonday silence, in order not to see with physical eyes nor hear with corporeal ears. Then . . . the dead awoke, and Pompeii began to live again." While thus, by means of his imagination, he endows the past with life, he suddenly sees what is unmistakably the Gradiva of his bas-relief step out of a house and walk buoyantly over the lava steppingstones to the other side of the street, just as he had seen her in the dream that night when she had lain down to sleep on the steps of the Temple of Apollo. "With this memory he became conscious, for the first time, of something else; he had, without himself knowing the motive in his heart, come to Italy on that account, and had, without stop, continued from Rome and Naples to Pompeii to see if he could here find any trace of her (and that in a literal sense), for, with her unusual gait, she must have left behind in the ashes a footprint different from all the others."

The suspense in which the author of *Gradiva* has kept us up to this point mounts here, for a moment, to embarrassing confusion. Not only has our hero apparently lost his equilibrium, but we, too, are lost when we are confronted with the appearance of Gradiva, who was formerly a plaster cast and then a creation of imagination. Is it a hallucination of our deluded hero, a "real" ghost, or a corporeal person? Not that we need to believe in ghosts to draw up this list. Jensen, who called his tale a "Fancy," has, of course, found no occasion as yet to explain to us whether he wishes to leave us in our world, decried as dull and ruled by the laws of science, or to conduct us into another fantastic one, in which reality is given to ghosts and spirits. As *Hamlet* and *Macbeth* show, we are ready to follow him to such a place without hesitation. The delusion of the imaginative archaeologist would have to be measured by another standard in that case. Indeed, when we consider how improbable must be the real existence of a woman who faithfully reproduces in her appearance that antique bas-relief, our list boils down to an alternative: hallucination or ghost of the noon hour. A slight touch in the description eliminates the former possibility. A large lizard lies stretched out, motionless, in the sunlight; it flees, however, before the approaching foot of Gradiva and wriggles away over the lava pavement. Hence, there is no hallucination, but something outside the senses of our dreamer. But should the reality of a *rediviva* be capable of disturbing a lizard?

Before the house of Meleager, Gradiva disappears. We are not surprised that Norbert Hanold persists in his delusion that Pompeii has begun to live again about him in the noon hour of spirits and that Gradiva has also returned to life and gone into the house where she lived before that fateful August day of the year 79. There dart through his mind keen conjectures about the personality of the owner, after whom the house may have been named, and about Gradiva's relation to the latter; these show that his science has now completely entered the service of his imagination. After stepping inside this house, he again suddenly discovers the apparition, sitting on low steps between two yellow pillars. "Spread out on her knees lay something white which he was unable to distinguish clearly; it seemed to be a papyrus sheet." Taking for granted his most recent suppositions about her ancestry, he speaks to her in Greek, awaiting timorously the determination of whether the power of speech may be granted to her in her phantom existence. As she does not answer, he changes the greeting to Latin. Then, from smiling lips, come the words, "If you wish to speak with me, you must do so in German."

What embarrassment for us, the readers! So the author of *Gradiva* has made sport of us and decoyed us, as if by means of the refulgence of Pompeiian sunshine, into a little delusion, so that we might be more lenient in our judgment of the poor man upon whom the real noonday sun is actually burning down; but we know now, after recovering from brief confusion, that Gradiva is a living German girl, a fact which we were just about to reject as utterly improbable. In control once more, we may now calmly wait to learn what

connection there is between the girl and the stone representation of her and how our young archaeologist acquired the
fantasies which hint at her real personality.

Our hero is not freed from the delusion as quickly as we
are, for, "even if the belief brought happiness," says our
author, "a considerable amount of incomprehensibility had
to be put up with." Besides, this delusion probably has subjective roots of which we know nothing, which do not exist
in us. Our hero probably needs radical treatment to bring
him back to reality. For the present he can do nothing but
adapt the delusion to the wonderful discovery which he has
just made. Gradiva, who perished at the destruction of
Pompeii, can be nothing but a ghost of the noon hour who
returns to life for the brief noon hour of spirits. But why,
after the answer given in German, does the exclamation
escape him: "I knew that your voice would sound like that"?
Not only we, but the girl, too, must ask that question, and
Hanold must admit that he has never heard her voice before, but expected to hear it in the dream, when he called
to her, as she was lying down to sleep on the steps of the
temple. He begs her to repeat that action, but she rises,
directs a strange glance at him, and, after a few steps, disappears between the pillars of the court. A beautiful butterfly had, shortly before that, fluttered about her a few times;
in his interpretation it had been a messenger from Hades,
who was to admonish the departed one to return, as the
noon hour of spirits had passed. Hanold manages to cry
after the disappearing girl: "Are you coming here again
tomorrow in the noon hour?" To us, however, who venture
to give more sober interpretations now, it would seem as
though the young lady found something improper in the

request which Hanold had made of her and therefore, insulted, left him, since she could not have known about
his dream. Might not her delicacy of feeling have sensed
the erotic nature of the request, which, for Hanold, was
prompted only by the connection with his dream?

After the disappearance of Gradiva, our hero examines all
the guests present in the dining room of the Hotel Diomed
and afterwards does likewise at the Hotel Suisse; he can
then assure himself that in neither of the only two lodgings
known to him in Pompeii is there a person to be found who
possesses the remotest resemblance to Gradiva. Of course,
he would have rejected as absurd the supposition that he
might really meet Gradiva in one of the two hostelries. The
wine pressed on the hot soil of Vesuvius then helps to increase the dizziness in which he has spent the day.

The only certainty about the next day is that Norbert
must again be in Meleager's house at noon; and, awaiting
the hour, he enters Pompeii over the old city wall—a way
which is against the rules. An asphodel stalk with white bell-
like blossoms seems to him, as flower of the underworld, significant enough to pluck and carry away. While he is waiting, however, all classical scholarship seems to him the
most purposeless and indifferent matter in the world, for
another interest has taken hold of him, the problem of
"what is the nature of the physical manifestation of a being
like Gradiva, dead and alive at the same time, although the
latter is true only in the noon hour of spirits." He is also wor-
ried lest today he may not meet the lady sought, because
perhaps she may not be allowed to return for a long time;
and when he sees her again between the pillars, he considers her appearance a figment of his imagination, which

draws from him the grieved exclamation, "Oh, that you were still alive!" This time, however, he has evidently been too critical, for the apparition possesses a voice which asks him whether he wishes to bring her the white flower and draws the man, who has again lost his composure, into a long conversation. Our author informs us, the readers, to whom Gradiva has already become interesting as a living personality, that the ill-humor and aloofness expressed in her eyes on the previous day have given way to an expression of searching curiosity and inquisitiveness. She really sounds him out, demands an explanation of his remark of the preceding day as to when he had stood near her as she was lying down to sleep; in this way she learns of the dream in which she perished with her native city, then of the bas-relief and the position of the foot which so attracted the young archaeologist. Now she shows herself ready to demonstrate her manner of walking; here the substitution for the sandals of light, sand-colored shoes of fine leather, something that she explains as an adaptation to the present, is established as the only deviation from the original relief of Gradiva. She is apparently going along with his delusion, the whole range of which she elicits from him without once contradicting him. Only once does she appear to be deflected from her play-acting by her emotions when he asserts, with his mind on the bas-relief, that he has recognized her at first glance. Since she knows nothing as yet of the relief at this stage of the conversation, it would be natural for her to misunderstand Hanold's words, but she presently has herself under control again, and only to us do many of her speeches appear to have a double meaning—a real and present meaning in addition to their significance in con-

nection with the delusion, as, for example, when she regrets
that he did not succeed in confirming the Gradiva gait on
the street. "What a shame," she says; "perhaps you would
not have needed to take the long journey here." She learns
also that he has named the bas-relief of her "Gradiva," and
tells him that her real name is Zoë.

"The name suits you beautifully, but it sounds to me like
bitter mockery, for 'Zoë' means 'life.'"

"One must resign oneself to the inevitable," she responds.
"And I have long accustomed myself to being dead."

With the promise to be at the same place again on the
morrow, she takes leave of him, but not before she has
asked for and received the asphodel cluster. "To those who
are more fortunate one gives roses in spring, but for me the
flower of oblivion is the right one from your hand." Presumably, melancholy is suited to one so long dead who has
returned to life for but a few short hours.

We begin now to understand and to hope. If the young
lady, in whose form Gradiva is again revived, accepts
Hanold's delusion so completely, she probably does it to free
him from it. No other course is open; by opposition one
would destroy that possibility. Even the serious treatment
of a real condition of this kind could proceed no differently
than to place itself first on the ground floor of the delusion-
structure and then to investigate it as thoroughly as possible.
If Zoë is the right person, we shall soon learn how one cures
delusions like those of our hero. We should also like to
know how such a delusion originates. It would be strange
indeed, and yet not without example and parallel, if the
treatment and the investigation of the delusion should
coincide and, while it is being analyzed, result in the ex-

planation of its origin. We have a suspicion, of course, that our case might then boil down to an "ordinary" love story, but one must not scorn love as a curative power for delusion; and was not our hero's captivation by the Gradiva-relief also a complete infatuation, still directed, to be sure, at the bygone and lifeless?

After Gradiva's disappearance, there is heard once more a distant sound like the merry note of a bird flying over the city of ruins. The man who has remained behind picks up something white, which Gradiva has left—not a papyrus leaf, but a sketchbook with pencil drawings of various scenes of Pompeii. We should say that the fact that she has forgotten the little book in this place is a pledge of her return, for we maintain that one forgets nothing without a secret reason or a hidden motive.

The remainder of the day brings our hero all sorts of strange discoveries and observations which he neglects to fit together. In the wall of the portico where Gradiva disappeared he notices today a narrow cleft which, however, is wide enough to afford passage to an unusually slender figure. He realizes that Zoë need not sink into the ground here— an idea which is so contrary to reason that he is now ashamed of his discarded belief—but that she uses this route to get back to her tomb. A faint shadow seems to him to dissolve at the end of the Street of Tombs, in front of the so-called Villa of Diomede. Dizzy, as on the previous day, and occupied with the same problems, he now roves about Pompeii, wondering about the physical nature of Zoë-Gradiva and whether one would feel anything if one touched her hand. A peculiar impulse urges him to undertake this experiment, and yet an equally great timidity restrains him from the very idea.

On a hot, sunny slope he meets an elderly man who, judging by his equipment, must be a zoologist or a botanist and seems to be busy catching things. The man turns to him and says: "Are you interested in *Faraglionensis*, too? I should hardly have supposed it, but to me it seems not at all unlikely that it not only dwells in the *Faraglioni* of Capri, but also can with some perseverance be found on the mainland. The method suggested by my colleague, Eimer, is really good; I have already used it often with the best of success. Please keep quite still." The speaker stops talking then and holds a little snare, made of a long blade of grass, in front of a narrow crevice from which the blue, chatoyant little head of a lizard peeps. Hanold leaves the lizard-hunter with the critical thought that it is hard to believe what odd and crazy projects can cause people to take that long trip to Pompeii—a criticism in which he does not, of course, include himself and his intention of seeking footprints of Gradiva in the ashes of Pompeii. The gentleman's face, moreover, seems familiar to him, as if he had noticed it casually in one of the two hotels; the man's manner of addressing him also sounded as if directed at an acquaintance.

As he continues his wandering, a side street leads him to a house he has not previously discovered; this turns out to be the "Albergo del Sole." The hotelkeeper, who is not busy, avails himself of the opportunity to recommend highly his house and the excavated treasures in it. He asserts that he was present when there were found near the Forum the young lovers who, on realizing their inevitable doom, had clasped each other in a firm embrace and thus awaited death. Hanold has already heard that story before and shrugged his shoulders over it as a fabulous invention of some especially imaginative storyteller; but today the words of the hotel-keeper inspire in him a credulity which even increases when the former produces a metal brooch encrusted with green patina, which, he claims, was gathered from the ashes along with the remains of the girl. Hanold acquires this brooch without further hesitation, and when, on leaving the hotel, he sees a cluster of asphodel blossoms nodding down from an open window, the sight of the grave-flower thrills him as an attestation of the genuineness of his new possession.

With this brooch, however, a new delusion has taken possession of him—or, rather, the old one has acquired an offshoot, apparently not a good omen for the therapy which has been started. Not far from the Forum a couple of young lovers were excavated in an embrace, and in the dream he saw Gradiva lie down to sleep in that very neighborhood, at the Temple of Apollo. Was it not possible that in reality she went still farther than the Forum in order to meet someone with whom she then died?

A tormenting feeling, which we can perhaps equate with jealousy, originates from this supposition. He appeases it by referring to the uncertainty of the connections, and regains his senses to the extent of being able to have his evening meal in the Hotel Diomede. His attention is attracted by two newly arrived guests, a man and a woman, whom, because of a certain resemblance, he takes for brother and sister—in spite of the difference in the color of their hair. They are the first people he has encountered on this trip who seem possibly congenial. A red Sorrento rose, which the young girl wears, awakes in him some memory—he cannot recall what. Finally he goes to bed and dreams; it is oddly nonsensical stuff, but obviously concocted of the day's experiences. "Somewhere in the sun Gradiva sat making a trap out of a blade of grass, in order to catch a lizard, and she said: 'Please stay quite still—my colleague is right; the method is really good, and she has used it with the greatest success!'" He resists the dream, even in his sleep, with the criticism that it is, of course, utter madness, and he succeeds in getting rid of it with the aid of an invisible bird that utters a short, merry call and carries the lizard away in its beak.

In spite of all this ghostly visitation, he awakes, if anything, with his mind cleared and settled. A rose bush, which bears flowers of the kind that he noticed yesterday on the young lady, recalls to him that in the night someone said that in the spring one gave roses. Instinctively, he plucks some of the roses, and there must be some association with these which has a liberating effect on his mind. Rid of his aversion to human beings, he takes the customary road to Pompeii, laden with the roses, the brooch, and the sketchbook, and occupied by the various problems relating to Gradiva. The old delusion has become full of flaws; he already doubts if she is permitted to stay in Pompeii in the noon hour only and not at other times. However, the emphasis has now shifted to the latest addition to his delusion, and the jealousy connected with it torments him in all sorts of disguises. He almost wishes that the apparition should remain visible only to his eyes and escape the notice of others; in that way, he might consider her his exclusive property. During his ramble awaiting the noon hour he has a surprising encounter. In the Casa del Fauno he happens upon two people who doubtless believe themselves undiscoverable in a nook, for they are embracing each other and their lips meet. With amazement he recognizes in them the congenial couple of yesterday evening; but for brother and sister their present position, the embrace and the kiss, seem to him of too long duration. So it is a couple of lovers after all, probably a young honeymoon couple, another Augustus and Gretchen. And timidly, as if he had disturbed a secret act of devotion, he withdraws unobserved. A feeling of deference which has long been lacking in him has been restored.

Arriving at the house of Meleager, he is beset by such fear that he may find Gradiva in the company of another man that he can find no other greeting for her than the question: "Are you alone?" With difficulty she makes him realize that he has picked the roses for her; he confesses to her his latest delusion, that she is the girl who was found in the Forum in her lover's embrace and to whom the green brooch had belonged. Not without mockery she inquires if, by any chance, he found the piece in the sun; the latter—here called "Sole" —produces many things of that sort. As a cure for the dizziness which he admits, she proposes that he share her lunch with her and offers him half of a piece of white bread wrapped in tissue paper; the other half of this she consumes with obvious appetite. As she eats, her faultless teeth gleam between her lips and, in biting the crust, make a slight crunching sound. He does not know how to reply to her remark, "It seems to me as if we had eaten our bread together like this once, two thousand years ago"; but the strengthening of his mind by the nourishment and all the evidences of present time that she gives do not fail to have an effect upon him. Reason stirs in him and makes him doubt the whole delusion that Gradiva is only a noonday ghost; on the other hand, there is the objection that she herself has just said that she had already shared her meal with him two thousand years ago. As a means of settling this conflict there occurs to him an experiment which he executes with slyness and regained courage. Her left hand, with its slender fingers, is resting on her knees, and one of those houseflies at whose boldness and uselessness he formerly became so indignant alights on this hand. Suddenly Hanold's hand rises and, with no gentle stroke, comes down on the fly and on Gradiva's hand. This daring experiment yields him twofold success: first, the joyous conviction that he has definitely touched a really living, warm hand; then, however, a reprimand which makes him start up in terror from his seat on the step. For, after Gradiva has recovered from her amazement, these words come from her lips: "You are obviously crazy, Norbert Hanold."

Calling a person by name is recognized as the best method of awakening someone who is sleeping or a somnambulist. Unfortunately we are not permitted to observe the results, for Norbert Hanold, of Gradiva's calling his name, which he had told to no one in Pompeii. For at this critical moment, the congenial lovers appear from the Casa del Fauno, and the young lady cries, in a tone of pleasant surprise, "Zoë! You here, too? And also on your honeymoon? You haven't written me a word about it, you know." At this new proof of the living reality of Gradiva, Hanold takes flight.

Zoë-Gradiva, too, is none too pleasantly surprised at the unexpected visit which disturbs her, it seems, in an important piece of work. Soon composed, she answers the question with a glib speech in which she informs her friend, and even more us, about the situation; and thereby she succeeds in getting rid of the young couple. She offers them her congratulations, but says that she herself is not on her wedding trip. "The young man who just went away is also laboring under a strange delusion; it seems to me that he believes a fly is buzzing in his head; well, everybody probably has some kind of bee in his bonnet. As is my duty, I have some knowledge of entomology and can, therefore, be of a little service in such cases. My father and I are staying at the 'Sole'; he, too, had a sudden attack and, on top of that, the good idea of bringing me here with him if I agreed to be responsible for my own entertainment and to make no demands upon him. I said to myself that I should certainly dig up something interesting here by myself. Of course, I certainly didn't expect the find which I made—I mean the good fortune of meeting you, Gisa."

Zoë now feels obliged to leave at once, to keep her father company at the "Sole." So she leaves, after she has introduced herself to us as the daughter of the zoologist and lizard-catcher and has admitted, in various ambiguous phrases, her therapeutic intentions and other secret ones. The direction which she takes is not that of the Sun Hotel, where her father is waiting for her, but it seems to her, too, that in the region of the Villa of Diomede a shadowy form is seeking her burial-place and disappearing under one of the monuments; therefore, with foot poised each time almost perpendicularly, she directs her steps to the Street of Tombs. This is where Hanold has fled, in shame and confusion, and is wandering up and down in the portico of the court without stopping, occupied with settling the rest of his problems through mental effort. One thing has become unimpeachably clear to him: that he was utterly foolish and irrational to believe that he communed with a young Pompeiian girl who had become more or less physically alive again; and this clear insight into his madness is incontestably an essential bit of progress in his return to sound reason. On the other hand, this living girl, with whom other people, too, communicate as with one of a corporeal reality like theirs, is Gradiva, and she knows his name; to solve this riddle his scarcely awakened reason is not strong enough. Emotionally, too, he is hardly calm enough to be equal to so difficult a task, for he would like best to have been buried two thousand years ago in the Villa of Diomede, only to be sure of never meeting Zoë-Gradiva again. A violent longing to see her again struggles meanwhile with the remnants of the inclination to flee, which has persisted in him.

Turning one of the four corners of the colonnade, he suddenly recoils. On a fragmentary wall-ruin there sits one of the girls who met death here in the Villa of Diomede. But this last attempt to take refuge again in the realm of madness is soon put aside; no, it is Gradiva, who has apparently come to give him the last bit of her treatment. She correctly interprets his first instinctive movement as an attempt to leave the place, and points out to him that he cannot escape, for a frightful cloudburst is in progress outside. The merciless girl begins the examination with the question as to what he intended in connection with the fly on her hand. He does not have the courage to make use of a certain pronoun,[2] but does have the more valuable kind needed to ask the decisive question.

[2] [I.e., for *you*, the familiar *du* rather than the formal *Sie*.—TRANS.]

"I was—as someone said—somewhat confused in my head and beg pardon that I—the hand—like that—how I could be so stupid I can't understand—but I can't understand either how its owner could use my name in upbraiding me for my—my unreason."

"So your power of understanding has not yet progressed that far, Norbert Hanold. Of course, I cannot be surprised, for you have long ago accustomed me to it. To have that experience again, I need not have come to Pompeii, and you could have confirmed it for me a good hundred miles nearer."

A good hundred miles nearer. "Diagonally across from your house, in the corner house; in my window there is a cage with a canary in it," she discloses to the still uncomprehending man.

This last reference strikes the listener like a memory from afar. That is surely the same bird whose song suggested the trip to Italy to him.

"In that house lives my father, Richard Bertgang, professor of Zoology."

As his neighbor, therefore, she is acquainted with him and his name. The disappointment of a superficial solution seems to be threatening us, a solution unworthy of our expectations.

As yet Norbert Hanold shows no regained independence of thought, when he repeats: "Then are you—are you Miss Zoë Bertgang? But she looked quite different—"

Miss Bertgang's answer then shows that other relations besides those of neighborliness have existed between them. She knows how to intercede for the familiar manner of address, which he has, of course, used toward the noonday spirit, but withdrawn again from the living girl; she now lays claim to former privileges. "If you find that form of address more suitable between us, I can use it, too, of course, but the other came to me more naturally. I don't know whether I looked different once, when we used to run about together as friends every day and occasionally beat and cuffed each other for a change; but if, in recent years, you had favored me with even one glance, you might perhaps have noticed that I have looked like this for a long time."

So a childhood friendship had existed between the two, perhaps a childhood love, from which derived the justification for the familiar form of address. Isn't this solution perhaps as superficial as the one first supposed? But it occurs to us that this childhood relationship explains in an unexpected way so many details of what has occurred between them in their present association—which makes the matter much deeper. Does it not seem that the blow on Zoë-Gradiva's hand, which Norbert Hanold has so splendidly motivated by the need to solve experimentally the question of the physical existence of the apparition, is, from another standpoint, strangely similar to a revival of the impulse for "beating and cuffing," whose sway in childhood Zoë's words have testified to? And when Gradiva asks the archaeologist whether it does not seem to him as if they had already shared their luncheon once, two thousand years ago, does not the incomprehensible question suddenly become meaningful if we substitute for the historical past the personal childhood, whose memories persist vividly for the girl, but seem to have been forgotten by the young man? Does not the idea suddenly dawn upon us that the fantasies of the young man about his Gradiva may be an echo of these forgotten childhood memories? Then they would be no arbitrary productions of his imagination, but determined, without his knowing it, by the existing material of childhood impressions already forgotten, but still active in him. We ought to be able to point out in detail the origin of these fantasies, even if only by conjecture. If, for instance, Gradiva simply must be of *Greek* ancestry, the daughter of a respected man, perhaps of a priest of Ceres, this would agree rather well with an aftereffect of the knowledge of her Greek name, *Zoë*, and of her membership in the family of a professor of Zoology. If, however, these fancies of Hanold's are transformed memories, we may expect to find in the disclosures of Zoë Bertgang an indication of the sources of these fancies. Let us listen; she was telling us of an intimate childhood friendship; we shall soon learn what further development this childhood relation had in both.

"In those days, up to the time when people, for some unknown reason, call us 'Backfisch,'[3] I had really acquired a strange attachment for you and thought that I could never find a more congenial friend in the world. I had no mother, sister, or brother, you know; to my father, a slowworm in alcohol was far more interesting than I, and people (I count girls among them) must surely have something with which they can occupy their thoughts and whatever else is connected with these. You were that something in those days. But when archaeology had come over you, I made the discovery that you—excuse me for using the familiar form of address, but your new formality sounds too absurd to me; besides, it isn't suitable for what I want to express—as I

[3] [*Backfisch*, literally "fish for frying" or "fried fish," is a term commonly applied to adolescent girls.—TRANS.]

was saying, it turned out that you had become an unbearable person who no longer had, at least for me, an eye in his head, a tongue in his mouth, nor a memory in his head, which is the place where I retain *my* memories of our childhood friendship. So I probably looked different from what I did formerly, for when I occasionally met you at a party, as recently as last winter, you did not look at me and I did not hear your voice; in this, of course, there was nothing that marked me out especially, for you treated all the others in the same way. To you I was but air, and you, with your shock of light hair, which I had once upon a time mussed up so often, were as boring, shriveled-up, and tongue-tied as a stuffed cockatoo and at the same time as grandiose as an—*archaeopteryx;* I think that's the name of that excavated antediluvian bird-monster. But that your head harbored an imagination so magnificent as to consider me, here in Pompeii, as something excavated and restored to life—that I had not surmised of you. And when you suddenly stood before me unexpectedly, it cost me some effort at first to understand what kind of incredible fancy your imagination had invented. Then I was amused and, in spite of its madness, it was not entirely displeasing to me. For, as I said, I had not expected it of you."

Thus she tells us clearly enough what has, over the years, become of the childhood friendship for both of them. With her it expanded into an intense love affair, for a girl must have something or someone to give her heart to. Miss Zoë, the incarnation of cleverness and clarity, makes her psychic life, too, quite transparent for us. If it is the general rule for a normal girl to turn her affection first to her father, Zoë was especially ready to do it, she who had no one but her father in her family; but this father cared nothing for her; the objects of his science had captured all his interest. So she had to look around for another person and clung with special fervor to the playmate of her youth. When he, too, no longer had any eyes for her, it did not destroy her love, but rather increased it, for he had become like her father, like him absorbed by science and, by it, isolated from life and from Zoë. So it was granted to her to be faithful even in unfaithfulness, to find her father again in her beloved, to embrace both with the same feeling, or, as we may say, to make them both identical in her emotions.

Where do we get the justification for this little psychological analysis, which may easily seem autocratic? In a single, but intensely characteristic, detail the author of the romance gives it to us. When Zoë pictures for us the transformation of the playmate of her youth, which seems so sad for her, she insults him by a comparison with the archaeopteryx, that bird-monster which belongs in the archaeology of zoology. Thus she has found a single concrete expression for the identification of both men; her resentment strikes the beloved as well as the father with the same word. The archaeopteryx is, so to speak, the compromise or intermediary concept in which the folly of her beloved coincides with her thought of the analogous folly of her father.

With the young man, things have taken a different turn. Classical scholarship took possession of him and left him an interest only in women of bronze and stone. The childhood friendship died, instead of developing into a passion, and the memories of it passed into such absolute forgetfulness that he does not recognize nor pay any attention to the friend of his youth when he meets her socially. Of course, when we consider further developments, we may doubt if "forgetfulness" is the right psychological term for the fate of these memories of our archaeologist. There is a kind of forgetting which distinguishes itself by the difficulty with which the memory is awakened, even by strong objective appeals, as if a subjective resistance struggled against the revival. Such forgetting has been termed "repression" in psychopathology; the case which Jensen has presented to us seems to be an example of repression. Now we do not generally know whether, in psychic life, forgetting an impression is connected with the destruction of its memory-trace; about repression, however, we can state with certainty that it does not coincide with the destruction, the obliteration, of the memory. The repressed material cannot, as a rule, break through of itself as a memory, but it does remain potent and effective. Some day, under external influence, it causes a series of psychic phenomena which one may regard as products of transformation or as offshoots of forgotten memories; if one does not view them as such, they remain incomprehensible. In Norbert Hanold's fantasies about Gradiva, we thought we recognized already the offshoots of the repressed memories of his childhood friendship with Zoë Bertgang. We may expect such a recurrence of the repressed material with special logical certainty if a person's erotic feelings are attached to the repressed ideas, if the erotic life has been involved in the repression. Then there is truth in the old Latin proverb which perhaps originally referred to expulsion through external influences, not to inner conflict: *Naturam furca expellas, semper redibit* (You may drive out natural disposition with a two-pronged fork, but it will always return). But it does not tell all, announces only the fact that repressed material does return, and does not describe at all the most peculiar manner of this recurrence, which is accomplished as if by a malicious betrayal. The very thing which has been chosen as a means of repression—like the "two-pronged fork" of the proverb—becomes the carrier of the thing recurring; in and behind the agencies of repression the material repressed finally asserts itself victoriously.

A well-known etching by Félicien Rops illustrates this fact (which is generally overlooked and lacks acceptance) more impressively than many explanations could; and he does it through the model case of repression in the lives of saints and penitents. An ascetic monk has sought refuge, most likely from the temptations of the world, near the image of the crucified Savior. Then, phantom-like, the cross sinks and, in its stead, there rises shining the image of a voluptuous, unclad woman, in the same position of the crucifixion. Other painters of less psychological insight have, in such representations of temptation, depicted sin as bold and triumphant and relegated it to some place near the Savior on the cross. Rops alone has allowed it to take the place of the Savior on the cross; he seems to have known that the thing repressed proceeds, at its recurrence, from the agency of repression itself.

In cases of illness it is worth one's while to observe at first hand how sensitive a patient's psychic life becomes in a state of repression to the approach of the repressed material; very subtle and slight resemblances suffice to activate it again behind the agencies of repression and through them. I once had occasion to treat a young man, still almost a boy, who, after his first unwelcome notice of sexual processes, had taken flight from all desires rising up in him and used various means for their repression: he increased his zeal for study, overemphasized his childlike attachment to his mother, and in general assumed childish ways. I shall not detail here how his repressed sexuality broke forth again especially in his relationship to his mother, but should like to describe the less common and stranger case of the breaking down of another of his bulwarks from a cause that can hardly be recognized as sufficient. Mathematics enjoys the greatest reputation as a distraction from sexual matters. J. J. Rousseau once had to listen to this advice from a lady who was dissatisfied with him: *"Lascia le donne e studia le matematiche"* ("Leave women alone and study mathematics"). Thus our fugitive tackled his mathematics and geometry in school with special zeal, until one day his mental powers weakened in the face of a few innocuous problems. The phrasing of two of these could still be determined: "Two bodies collide; one is traveling at a speed of . . ." And: "Inscribe a cone in a cylinder with the diameter $m$ . . ." Because of these allusions to the sexual act, which are certainly not obvious to others, the young man felt let down by mathematics, too, and took flight from it as well.

If Norbert Hanold were a living person who had, by means of archaeology, driven love and the memory of his childhood friendship out of his life, it would now be legitimate and correct that an antique relief should awaken in him the forgotten memory of the girl beloved in his childhood. It would be his well-deserved fate to have fallen in love with the stone representation of Gradiva, behind which, by virtue of an unexplained resemblance, the living and neglected Zoë becomes effective.

Miss Zoë herself seems to share our conception of the delusion of the young archaeologist, for the pleasure which she expresses at the end of her "unreserved, detailed, and instructive lecture" can be motivated only by his readiness to apply his interest in Gradiva to Zoë from the very beginning. This is exactly what she did not believe him capable of and what, in spite of all the disguises of the delusion, she recognizes as such. Her psychic treatment of him has had a salutary effect; he feels relieved, since the delusion has now been replaced by something of which it was only a distorted and unsatisfactory copy. He immediately remembers and recognizes her as his good, cheerful, level-headed comrade who has not changed essentially; but he finds something else most strange:

"To think that a person must first die to become alive," says the girl; "but for archaeologists that is necessary, I suppose." She has apparently not yet forgiven him for the detour which he made from the childhood friendship via classical scholarship to the relationship which is now establishing itself.

"No, I mean your name. . . . Because *Bertgang* has the same meaning as *Gradiva* and signifies 'the one splendid in walking.' "

Even we were not prepared for that. Our hero begins to rise from his humiliation and to play an active role. He is apparently completely cured of his delusion, lifted above it, and proves this by tearing asunder, on his own, the last threads of the web of delusion. Patients, too, act in just this way once the compulsion of their delusion has been broken by the disclosure of the repression behind it. Once they have understood, they themselves offer the solutions for the last and most significant riddles of their strange condition in suddenly emerging insights. We had already believed, of course, that the Greek ancestry of the mythical Gradiva was a dim aftereffect of the Greek name *Zoë*, but we did not dare to tackle the name *Gradiva* itself. We supposed it the free creation of Norbert Hanold's imagination—and behold! This very name now turns out to be an offshoot, in fact, the translation of the repressed family name of the supposedly forgotten beloved of his youth.

The derivation and dissolution of the delusion are now completed. What the author gives us from this point on may well serve as a harmonious conclusion of the story. With a view to the future, it can only strike us as pleasant if the rehabilitation of the man, who formerly had to play the lamentable role of one needing to be cured, progresses, and if he succeeds in arousing in the girl some of the emotions which he experienced previously. Thus it happens that he makes her jealous by mentioning the congenial young lady who disturbed them in the house of Meleager and by confessing that she was the first girl who had impressed him very much. When Zoë is then about to take a cool departure, remarking that now everything has become sensible again, she herself not least of all, and that he might look up Gisa Hartleben, or whatever her name might be now, and be of scientific assistance to her with the purpose of her stay in Pompeii; when she says that she must now go to the "Albergo del Sole" where her father is already waiting for her at lunch, and adds that perhaps they may see each other again sometime at a party in Germany or on the moon—then he once again seizes upon the troublesome fly as a means of taking possession first of her cheek and then of her lips, and takes the offensive, which simply is the man's duty in the game of love. Only once more does a shadow seem to fall on their happiness, when Zoë reminds him that now she must really go to her father who will otherwise starve in the "Sole."

"Your father—what will he—?"

But the clever girl knows how to silence this apprehension quickly. "Probably he will do nothing; I am not an indispensable piece in his zoological collection; if I were, my heart would perhaps not have clung to you so unwisely." However, should the father, by way of exception, want to have an opinion different from hers in this case, there is a sure method. Hanold needs only to go over to Capri, there catch a *lacerta faraglionensis* (the technique for which he may practice on her little finger), then set the animal free again here, catch it before the eyes of the zoologist, and give him the choice of the *faraglionensis* on the mainland or his daughter—a proposal in which, as one may easily note, mockery is combined with bitterness, an admonition to the betrothed, as it were, not to follow too closely the model after which his beloved has chosen him.

Norbert Hanold reassures us on this matter, too, by expressing, through all sorts of seemingly trivial symptoms, the great transformation that he has undergone. He voices his intention of taking a wedding trip with his Zoë to Italy and Pompeii, as if he had never been indignant at the newly married travelers, Augustus and Gretchen. His resentment against these happy couples, who so unnecessarily traveled more than one hundred miles from their German homes, has entirely disappeared. Certainly the author is right in pre-

senting such weakening of memory as the most valuable
sign of a mental change. Zoë replies to the announced desire
as to the destination of their journey, *"by her childhood
friend who had, in a way, also been excavated from the
ashes,"* that she does not yet feel quite alive enough to make
such a geographical decision.

Beautiful reality has now triumphed over the delusion;
yet an honor still awaits the latter before the two leave
Pompeii. When they have arrived at the gate of Hercules,
where, at the beginning of the Strada Consolare, old steppingstones cross the street, Norbert Hanold stops and asks
the girl to go ahead. She understands him and, "raising
her dress slightly with her left hand, Gradiva *rediviva* Zoë
Bertgang, viewed by him with dreamily observing eyes,
crossed with her calmly buoyant walk, through the sunlight,
over the steppingstones." With the triumph of eroticism,
there is an acknowledgment of what was beautiful and valuable in the delusion.

With the last metaphor of "the childhood friend excavated
from the ashes," the author of the story has, however, put
into our hand the key to the symbolism which the delusion
of the hero made use of in the disguise of the repressed
memory. There is no better analogy for repression, which at
the same time makes inaccessible and conserves something
psychic, than the burial which was the fate of Pompeii and
from which the city was able to rise again through work
with the spade. Therefore, in his imagination the young
archaeologist had to transport to Pompeii the prototype of
the relief which reminded him of the forgotten beloved of
his youth. Jensen, however, had a good right to linger over

the significant resemblance, which his fine sense had traced out, between a bit of psychic occurrence in an individual and a single historical event in the history of mankind.

## II

It was really our intention to investigate with the aid of certain analytical methods only the two or three dreams which are found in the tale *Gradiva;* how did it happen, then, that we allowed ourselves to be carried away to do an analysis of the whole story and an examination of the psychic processes of the two chief characters? Well, this was no superfluous work, but a necessary preparation. Even when we wish to understand the real dreams of an actual person, we must concern ourselves intensively with the character and the fortunes of this person, not only his experiences shortly before the dream, but also those of the remote past. In fact, I think that even now we are not free to turn to our real task, but must still linger over the piece of fiction itself and do more preparatory work.

Our readers will have noticed with raised eyebrows that until now we have considered Norbert Hanold and Zoë Bertgang in all their psychic manifestations and activities as if they were real individuals and not creatures of a writer, as if the mind of the author were absolutely transparent and not a refractory and cloudy medium; and our procedure must seem all the more surprising when we consider that the author expressly disavows the portrayal of reality by calling his tale a *Fancy.* We find, however, such a faithful copy of reality in all his descriptions that we should not voice any objections if *Gradiva* were called, not a *Fancy,* but a study in psychiatry.

Only in two instances has Wilhelm Jensen made use of his license to create suppositions which do not seem to be rooted in the causality of real life: first, when he has the young archaeologist find a genuinely antique bas-relief which, not only in the peculiar position of the foot in walking, but in all details, the shape of the face, and the bearing, copies a person living much later, so that he can consider the physical manifestation of this person to be the cast endowed with life; second, when the hero is caused to meet the living girl, of all places, in Pompeii, whither his fancy has transported the dead girl, while he separates himself, by the journey to Pompeii, from the living girl whom he has noticed on the streets of his home town. However, this second instance is no violent deviation from the possibilities of life; it simply utilizes chance, which undeniably plays a part in so many human fates, and, moreover, gives it meaning, for this chance reflects the destiny which has decreed that through flight one is delivered over to the very thing that one is fleeing from.

More fantastic and entirely a product of the author's arbitrariness seems the first supposition on which all further incidents are based—namely, the detailed resemblance of the cast to the living girl. Here, moderation might have limited the conformity to the one trait of the position of the foot in walking. One might be tempted at this point to let one's own imagination play in order to establish a connection with reality. The name Bertgang could point to the fact that the women of that family had been distinguished, even in ancient times, by the characteristic of a beautiful gait, and by heredity the German Bertgangs were connected with those Greeks,[1] a woman of whose family had caused the ancient artist to capture in a bas-relief the peculiarity of her walk. However, since the individual variations in human structure are not independent of one another, and since the ancient types which we come upon in the collections actually emerge in our midst time and again, it would not be entirely impossible that a modern Bertgang should repeat again the form of her ancient forebear, even in all the other details of her physique. Inquiry of the author of the story as to the sources of this creation might well be wiser than such speculation; we should then have a good prospect of changing once more a bit of seeming arbitrariness into causality. But since we do not have access to the psychic life of the author, we leave him the uncurtailed right to base an absolutely true-to-life development on an improbable supposition—a right which Shakespeare, for example, has asserted in *King Lear*.

But otherwise, let us repeat, Wilhelm Jensen has given us an entirely correct study in psychiatry, by which we may measure our understanding of psychic life, a story of illness and cure which seems designed for the inculcation of certain fundamental teachings of medical psychology. Strange enough that he should have done this! What if, in reply to questioning, he should deny this intention? It is so easy to draw comparisons and to put constructions on things. Are we not rather the ones who have woven secret meanings, which were far from his mind, into the beautiful poetic tale? Possibly; we shall come back to that later. For the time being, however, we have tried to refrain from such a tenden-

---

[1] [Cf. below the last paragraph of Freud's appendix to the second edition.—TRANS.]

tious interpretation by reproducing the story, in almost every case, in the author's own words; thus we have had the author himself furnish text as well as commentary. Anyone who will compare our text with that of *Gradiva* will have to grant this.

Perhaps in the judgment of the great majority we are rendering our author a poor service when we declare his work to be a study in psychiatry. A writer is to avoid all contact with psychiatry, we are told, and leave to physicians the portrayal of morbid psychic conditions. In reality, no true creative writer has ever heeded this commandment. The portrayal of the psychic life of human beings is actually his very special domain; he has always been the precursor of science and of scientific psychology. The borderline between normal and morbid psychic conditions is, in a way, a conventional one, and, in another way, in such a state of flux that probably every one of us oversteps it many times in the course of a day. On the other hand, psychiatry would do wrong if it wanted to limit itself permanently to the study of those serious and sad illnesses which arise from serious disturbances of the delicate psychic apparatus. It has no less interest in the slighter and adjustable deviations from the normal which we cannot yet trace back farther than to disturbances in the interplay of psychic forces; indeed, it is only by means of these that it can understand mental health as well as the manifestations of serious illness. Thus the creative writer cannot evade the psychiatrist nor the psychiatrist the creative writer, and the poetic treatment of a theme from psychiatry may turn out correctly without loss of beauty. A case in point is the present imaginative representation of a story of illness and its treatment; we can survey it better after finishing the tale and relieving our own suspense. Now we shall reproduce it in the technical terms of our science; in doing this we should not be disturbed by the necessity to repeat what has already been related.

Norbert Hanold's condition is called a "delusion" often enough by the author of the story, and we, too, have no reason to reject this designation. We can state two chief characteristics of a "delusion" by which it is not exhaustively described, to be sure, but clearly differentiated from other disturbances. First, it belongs to that group of illnesses which do not directly affect the physical, but express themselves only through psychic symptoms; secondly, it is distinguished by the fact that "fantasies" have assumed control —that is, are believed and have acquired influence on actions. If we recall the journey to Pompeii to seek in the ashes the peculiarly formed footprints of Gradiva, we have here a splendid example of an act under the sway of a delusion. A psychiatrist would perhaps assign Norbert Hanold's delusion to the large group of paranoia and designate it as a "fetishistic erotomania," because falling in love with the bas-relief would be the most striking thing to him and because, to his conception which exaggerates everything, the young archaeologist's interest in the feet and foot-position of women must seem suspiciously like fetishism. However, all such designations and divisions of the different kinds of delusion according to content tend to be awkward and useless.[2]

An old-school psychiatrist would, moreover, stamp our hero as a degenerate, because he is a person capable, on

---

[2] The case N.H. would actually have to be designated as a hysterical rather than a paranoiac delusion. The symptoms of paranoia are missing here.

account of such strange predilections, of developing a delusion, and would investigate the heredity which has inexorably driven him to such a fate. In this, however, Jensen does not follow him, and with good reason. He wants to bring the hero closer to us to facilitate our achieving empathy with him; with the diagnosis of "degenerate," whether or not it may be justifiable scientifically, the young archaeologist is at once moved far away from us, for we, the readers, are normal people and the measure of humanity. The essential facts of heredity and constitution underlying this condition also concern the author of *Gradiva* little; instead, he is engrossed in the individual psychic state which can give rise to such a delusion.

In one important point Norbert Hanold acts quite differently from ordinary human beings. He has no interest in living women; science, which he serves, has taken this interest from him and transferred it to women of stone or bronze. Let us not consider this an unimportant peculiarity; it is really the basic premise of the narrative, for one day it happens that one such bas-relief claims for itself all the interest which would normally be due to living women, and a delusion is the result. Before our eyes there is then unfolded the story of how this delusion is cured by a fortunate set of circumstances, the interest transferred back from stone to a living girl. The author of the story does not allow us to trace the influences through which our hero begins to avoid women; he only suggests to us that such conduct is not explained by his predisposition which includes, rather, the need for a bit of fantasy—erotic fantasy, we might add. We learn later also that in his childhood he was no different from other children; at that time he was friendly with the little girl, was inseparable from her, shared his lunches with her, cuffed her, and let her muss him up. In such an attachment, such a combination of tenderness and aggression, is expressed the incomplete eroticism of child life whose effects are not shown until later, but then irresistibly, and which, during childhood, only physicians and creative writers recognize as eroticism. Our author gives us to understand clearly that he, too, sees it in that light, for he suddenly causes to awaken in his hero, on a suitable occasion, a lively interest in the gait and foot-position of women—an interest which must bring him into disrepute as a foot-fetishist among scholars as well as the ladies of his home town, but to us is necessarily derived from the memory of his childhood playmate. This girl was surely even as a child characterized by the beautiful walk with her foot almost perpendicular as she stepped out, and through the portrayal of this very gait an antique bas-relief later acquired great significance for Norbert Hanold. Incidentally, let us add immediately that the author of *Gradiva* is in complete agreement with science in regard to the derivation of the peculiar phenomenon of fetishism. Since the investigations by Binet we have really attempted to trace fetishism back to erotic impressions of childhood.

The condition of continued avoidance of women results in the personal qualification, or, as we say, the disposition, for the formation of a delusion; the development of psychic disturbance begins at the moment when a chance impression awakens the forgotten childhood experiences in which there are at least vestiges of erotic content. But "awakened" is certainly not the right term when we consider the further developments. We must reproduce our author's correct rep-

resentation in felicitous psychological terminology. On seeing the relief Norbert does not remember that he has seen
such a foot-position in the friend of his youth; he does not
remember at all, and yet the entire effect of the relief proceeds from such a connection with the impression of his
childhood. Thus the childhood impression is stirred, made
active, so that it begins to show effects, though it does not
appear in consciousness, but remains "unconscious," a term
which we now unavoidably use in psychopathology. This
term "unconscious" we should now like to see withdrawn
from all the arguments of philosophers and natural philosophers, which often have only etymological significance. For
psychic processes which are active and yet at the same time
do not come through into the consciousness of the person
concerned, we have at present no better term, and we mean
nothing else by "unconsciousness." If some thinkers wish to
dispute as unreasonable the existence of such an unconscious, we think they have never occupied themselves with
the psychic phenomena in question and are under the spell
of the common experience that everything psychic which is
active and intensive becomes, at the same time, conscious.
They have still to learn what Jensen knows very well—that
there are psychic processes which, despite the fact that they
are intensive and show vigorous activity, remain far removed from consciousness.

We said once that his memories of his childhood relations
with Zoë are in a state of "repression" in Norbert Hanold;
and we have called them "unconscious" memories. Here we
must give some attention to the relation between the two
technical terms which seem to coincide in meaning. It is not
hard to clear this up. "Unconscious" is the broader term,

"repressed" the narrower. Everything that is repressed is unconscious; but we cannot assert that everything unconscious is repressed. If Hanold, at the sight of the relief, had remembered his Zoë's manner of walking, then a formerly unconscious memory would at the same time have become active and conscious in him and would have shown that it was not formerly repressed. "Unconscious" is a purely descriptive term, in many respects indefinite and, so to speak, static. "Repressed" is a dynamic expression which takes into consideration the play of psychic forces and denotes that there is present an effort to express all psychic activities, among them that of becoming conscious, but also a counterforce, a resistance, which is able to prevent a part of these psychic activities, including, again, that of becoming conscious. It is characteristic of the repressed material that, in spite of its intensity, it cannot break through into consciousness. In Hanold's case, therefore, it was, from the appearance of the bas-relief on, a matter of a repressed unconscious—in short, of a repression.

What is repressed in Norbert Hanold are his memories of his childhood association with the girl who walks beautifully, but this is not yet the correct view of the psychological situation. We remain on the surface so long as we treat only of memories and ideas. The only things in psychic life that can be evaluated are, rather, the emotions. All psychic forces are significant only through their aptitude to arouse emotions. Ideas are repressed only because they are bound up with releases of emotions that are not to come about; it would be more correct to say that repression affects the emotions, but these are comprehensible to us only in their tie-up with ideas. Thus, in Norbert Hanold, the erotic feelings are repressed, and, since his eroticism neither knows nor has known another object than Zoë Bertgang in his youth, the memories of her are forgotten. The antique bas-relief awakens the slumbering eroticism in him and makes the childhood memories active. On account of a resistance in him to the eroticism, these memories can become active only as unconscious ones. What now happens in him is a struggle between the power of eroticism and the forces that are repressing it; the manifestation of this struggle is a delusion.

Our author has omitted to give the motive from which stems the repression of the erotic life in his hero. The latter's interest in science is, of course, only the means which the repression employs; a physician would have to probe deeper here, perhaps in this case without finding the foundation. However, the author of *Gradiva*, as we have admiringly emphasized, has not hesitated to represent to us how the awakening of the repressed eroticism results from the very sphere of the means which are serving the repression. It is rightly an antique, the bas-relief of a woman, through which our archaeologist is snatched out of his alienation from love and admonished to pay the debt with which all of us are charged from birth.

The first manifestations of the process now stimulated by the bas-relief are fantasies that play with the person represented by it. The model appears to him to be something "of the present," in the best sense, as if the artist had fixed the girl walking on the street "from life." He bestows upon the girl the name "Gradiva," which he forms from the epithet of the war-god advancing to battle, Mars Gradivus. He endows her personality with more and more details. She may be the daughter of an esteemed man, perhaps of a

patrician who is associated with the temple service of a
deity; he believes that he sees Greek ancestry in her features; and finally he feels impelled to transport her far away
from the confusion of a metropolis to more peaceful Pompeii, where he has her walking over the lava steppingstones
which make it possible to cross the street. These feats of
fantasy seem arbitrary enough and yet again harmless and
unsuspicious. Even when from them there is produced, for
the first time, the impulse to act—when the archaeologist,
oppressed by the problem of whether such a foot-position
corresponds to reality, begins observations from life and
looks at the feet of contemporary women and girls—this act
is covered by conscious, scientific motives, as if all his interest in the bas-relief of Gradiva had originated in his pro-
fessional work in archaeology.

The women and girls on the street, whom he uses as objects for his investigation, must, of course, have a different,
coarsely erotic conception of his conduct; and we must admit that they are right. For us, there is no doubt but that
Hanold knows as little about his motives as he does about
the origin of his fantasies concerning Gradiva. These latter
are, as we shall learn later, echoes of his memories of the beloved of his youth, offshoots of these memories, transformations and distortions of them that arose after they failed to
push into consciousness in unchanged form. The supposedly
aesthetic judgment that the relief represents "something of
the present" is substituted for the knowledge that such a
gait does belong to a girl known to him and crossing streets
*in the present;* behind the impression "from life" and the
fancy about her Greek traits there is hidden the memory
of her name *Zoë,* which, in Greek, means *life; Gradiva,* as

the man finally cured of the delusion tells us, is a good translation of her family name, *Bertgang,* which means "splendid or magnificent in walking"; the determinations about her father stem from the knowledge that Zoë Bertgang is the daughter of an esteemed instructor at the university, which can probably be translated into antique terms as temple service. Finally, his imagination transports her to Pompeii, not "because her calm, quiet manner seems to require it," but because in his science there is found no other or better analogy to the strange condition in which, through some obscure intimation, he senses his memories of his childhood friendship to be. Once he has equated his own childhood with the classical past—a natural thing for him to do—the interment of Pompeii, this disappearance plus preservation of the past, offers a striking resemblance to the *repression* of which he has knowledge by means of so-called "endopsychic" perception. The same symbolism, therefore, which the author has the girl use consciously at the end of the tale, is working in Hanold.

"I said to myself that I should certainly dig up something interesting here by myself. Of course, I didn't expect the find which I made." At the end, the girl replies to the announced desire as to the destination of the journey, "by her childhood friend who had, in a way, also been excavated from the ashes."

Thus we find in the very first manifestations of Hanold's fantasies and actions a twofold determination, a derivation from two different sources. One determination is the one which appears to Hanold himself; the other is the one which discloses itself to us upon examination of his psychic processes. One, the conscious one, is related to Hanold's person;

the other is entirely unconscious to him. One originates entirely from the ideational world of archaeological science; the other, however, proceeds from the repressed memories which have become active in him and the emotional impulses attached to them. The one seems superficial and covers up the other, which conceals itself behind the former, as it were. One might say that the scientific motivation serves the unconscious eroticism as a cloak and that science has placed itself completely at the service of the delusion; but one must not forget, either, that the unconscious determination can effect nothing but what is at the same time satisfactory to the conscious scientific one. The symptoms of delusion—fantasies as well as actions—are results of a compromise between the two psychic streams, and in a compromise the demands of each of the two parties are considered; each party has been obliged to forgo some part of what he wanted to carry out. Where a compromise has been established, there has been a struggle—here, the conflict assumed by us between the suppressed eroticism and the forces which keep it alive in the repression. In the formation of a delusion this struggle is never really ended.

Attack and resistance are renewed after every compromise-formation which, so to speak, is never quite sufficient. This our author also knows and therefore he causes a feeling of discontent, a peculiar restlessness, to dominate his hero in this phase of the disturbance, as a preliminary to and guarantee of further developments.

These significant peculiarities of the twofold determination for fantasies and decisions, of the formation of conscious pretexts for actions, for the motivation of which the re-

pressed has furnished the greater contribution, will, in the
further progress of the story, confront us repeatedly and perhaps even more clearly—and this rightfully, for in this
Jensen has grasped and represented the ever-present chief
characteristic of the morbid psychic processes. The development of Norbert Hanold's delusion progresses in a dream
which, caused by no new event, seems to proceed entirely
from his psychic life which is occupied by a conflict. But let
us pause before we proceed to test whether the author of
*Gradiva* meets our expectation of a deeper understanding
in the formation of his dreams, too. Let us first ask what
psychiatry has to say to his suppositions about the origin of
a delusion, how it stands on the matter of the role of repression and the unconscious, of conflict and compromise-formation. Briefly, can our author's representation of the genesis
of a delusion stand before the judgment of science?

And here we must give the perhaps unexpected answer
that, unfortunately, it is just the other way around: science
does not stand up before the accomplishment of our author.
Between the essential facts of heredity and constitution, and
the seemingly complete creations of delusion, science leaves
a gap which we find filled by the author of *Gradiva*. Science
does not yet recognize the significance of repression nor the
fact that it definitely needs the unconscious for an explanation of the world of psychopathological phenomena; it does
not seek the basis of delusion in psychic conflict and does
not regard its symptoms as a compromise-formation. Does
this mean that our author stands alone against science? It
does not—if the present writer may consider his own works
as part of science. For he himself has for a number of years

—and until recently almost alone[3]—represented all the views which he has culled from *Gradiva* by W. Jensen and presented here in technical terms. He has shown that the suppression of some impulses, together with the repression of the ideas by which a suppressed impulse is represented, is the predisposition for a psychic disturbance, and he has done so in greatest detail for the conditions known as hysteria and obsession; he has repeated the same view soon afterwards for many kinds of delusion.[4] Whether the impulses that may be involved in this causality are always components of the sex-impulse or might be of a different nature —this is a matter of indifference in the analysis of *Gradiva*, since in the case chosen by the author it is surely a matter only of the suppression of erotic feeling. The views concerning psychic conflict and the formation of symptoms by compromises between the two psychic forces struggling with each other—these the present writer has found valid in cases actually observed and professionally treated, in exactly the same way that he was able to observe them in Norbert Hanold, the invention of our author.[5] The tracing back of neurotic (especially hysterically morbid) activities to the influence of unconscious thoughts, P. Janet, the pupil of the great Charcot, had undertaken before the present writer,

[3] See the important work by E. Bleuler, *Affektivität, Suggestibilität, Paranoia* (Zurich, 1906), translated by Charles Ricksher in *New York State Hospitals Bulletin*, February 1912; and *Diagnostische Assoziationsstudien* by C. Jung (Zurich, 1906). [In the second edition (1912) Freud added: "Today this writer can reject the above works as no longer up to date. The 'psychoanalytic movement' inspired by him has greatly expanded since then and is still growing."—TRANS.]

[4] Cf. Freud, *Sammlung kleiner Schriften zur Neurosenlehre* (1906), translated in part by A. A. Brill in *Selected Papers on Hysteria and Other Psychoneuroses* (New York: Nervous and Mental Diseases Monograph No. 4, 1912).

[5] Cf. *Bruchstück einer Hysterie-Analyse* (1905).

who also made such studies in conjunction with Josef Breuer in Vienna.[6]

When the present writer devoted himself to such investigations of the origin of psychic disturbance in the years following 1893, it certainly did not occur to him to seek corroboration of his results in works of fiction. It therefore was no small surprise to him to learn that in *Gradiva,* published in 1903, a creative writer had based his creation on the very things that the present writer thought he was drawing, as something new, from the sources of medical experience. How had the author acquired the same knowledge as the physician, or, at any rate, what enabled him to behave as if he possessed it?

Norbert Hanold's delusion, we said, develops further through a dream which he has in the midst of his efforts to authenticate a gait like Gradiva's in the streets of his home town. The content of his dream we can outline briefly. The dreamer is in Pompeii on that day which brought destruction to the unfortunate city, experiences the horror without himself getting into danger, suddenly sees Gradiva walking there, and immediately understands as quite natural that, as she is a Pompeiian, she is living in her native city and "without his having any suspicion of it, was his contemporary." He is seized with fear for her and calls to her, whereupon she turns her face toward him momentarily. Yet she walks on without heeding him at all, lies down on the steps of the Temple of Apollo, and is buried by the rain of ashes, after her face has changed color as if it were turning to white marble, until it completely resembles a bas-relief.

[6] Cf. Breuer and Freud, *Studien über Hysterie* (1895), translated by A. A. Brill in *Selected Papers on Hysteria and Other Psychoneuroses.*

On awakening, he interprets the noises of the big city which reach his ear as the cries for help of the desperate inhabitants of Pompeii, and the booming of the turbulent sea. The feeling that what he has dreamed has really happened to him persists for some time after his awakening, and the conviction that Gradiva lived in Pompeii and died on that fatal day remains from this dream as an addition to his delusion.

It is less easy for us to say what the author of *Gradiva* intended by this dream and what caused him to connect the development of this delusion with a dream, of all things. Assiduous investigation of dreams has, to be sure, gathered enough evidence for the fact that mental disturbance is connected with and proceeds from dreams,[7] and even in the life-history of certain eminent men, impulses for important deeds and decisions are said to have been engendered by dreams. But our comprehension does not gain much by these analogies; let us therefore stick to our case, the case of the archaeologist, Norbert Hanold, a fiction of our author. At which end must one seize hold of such a dream to weave it into the context of the narrative, if it is not to remain an expendable adornment of fiction? I can imagine the reader exclaiming at this point: "The dream is easy to explain—a simple anxiety-dream, caused by the noise of the big city, which is given the new interpretation of the destruction of Pompeii by the archaeologist preoccupied with his Pompeiian girl!" Because of the commonly prevailing disdain of the achievements of dreams, one usually limits the demand for dream-explanation to seeking for a part of the dream-content an external excitation which may be equated with

[7] Cf. Sante de Sanctis, *I Sogni* (original in Italian), translated into German by Otto Schmidt, *Die Träume* (Halle, 1901).

it. This external excitation for the dream would be furnished
by the noise which wakens the sleeper; the interest in this
dream would be terminated thereby. Would that we had
even one reason to suppose that the metropolis had been
noisier than usual on this morning! If, for example, our author had only not omitted to inform us that Hanold had that
night, contrary to his custom, slept by an open window!
What a shame that the author did not take this trouble!
And if an anxiety-dream were only such a simple thing! No,
this interest is not terminated in such a simple way.

A connection with an external sensory stimulus is not
essential for dream-formation. The sleeper can neglect this
excitation from the outer world; he can let himself be awakened by it without forming a dream; he may also weave it
into his dream, as happens here, if it is of use to him from
any other motive; and there is an abundance of dreams for
whose content such a determination by a sensory excitation
of the sleeper cannot be shown. No, let us try another way.

Perhaps we can start from the residue which the dream
leaves in Hanold's waking life. It had formerly been his
fantasy that Gradiva was a Pompeiian. Now this assumption
becomes a certainty, and the second certainty is added that
she was buried there in the year 79. Sorrowful feelings ac-
company this progress of the formation of the delusion like
an echo of the fear which had filled the dream. This new
grief about Gradiva will seem to us not exactly comprehensible; Gradiva would now have been dead for many centuries
even if she had been saved from destruction in the year 79.
Or ought one to be permitted to argue in this way with
neither Norbert Hanold nor his creator? Here, too, no way
seems to lead to enlightenment. We wish, nevertheless, to

note that a markedly painful emotional element attaches to the augmentation which the delusion derives from this dream.

Otherwise, however, our perplexity is not dispelled. This dream does not explain itself; we must decide to borrow from *The Interpretation of Dreams* by the present writer and to apply some of the rules given there for the solution of dreams.

One of these rules is that a dream is regularly connected with the dreamer's activities on the day before. Our author seems to wish to intimate that he has followed this rule by connecting the dream directly with Hanold's "pedestrian investigations." Now the latter mean only a search for Gradiva, whom he expects to recognize by her characteristic manner of walking. The dream ought, therefore, to contain a reference to where Gradiva is to be found. It really does contain it by showing her in Pompeii, but that is nothing new to us.

Another rule says: If, after the dream, belief in the reality of the dream-images continues unusually long so that one cannot free himself from the dream, this is not a mistake in judgment called forth by the vividness of the dream-images, but a psychic act in itself, an assurance which refers to the dream-content, that something in it is as real as it has been dreamed to be; and one is right to believe this assurance. If we are guided by these two rules, we must decide that the dream gives information about the whereabouts of the sought-for Gradiva that coincides with reality. We now know Hanold's dream; does the application of these two rules lead to any sensible meaning?

Strange to say, it does. But this meaning is disguised in a special way, so that one does not recognize it immediately.

Hanold learns in the dream that the girl he is looking for lives in the city and in his own day. That is, of course, true of Zoë Bertgang, only that in his dream the city is not the German university city, but Pompeii, the time not the present, but the year 79, according to our reckoning. It is a kind of distortion by displacement; Gradiva is not transported to the present, but the dreamer is to the past; yet even this way we are given the essential and new fact that *he shares locality and time with the girl sought*. Whence, then, this dissimulation and disguise which must deceive us as well as the dreamer about the real meaning and content of the dream? Well, we already have means at hand to give us a satisfactory answer to this question.

Let us recall all that we have heard about the nature and origin of fantasies, these precursors of delusion. They are substitutes for and offshoots of repressed memories which some resistance does not allow to push into consciousness in unchanged form, but which manage to become conscious by heeding the censorship of resistance and undergoing transformations and distortions. After this compromise is completed, the former memories have become fantasies that may easily be misunderstood by the conscious person—that is, may be understood in the spirit of the dominant psychic current. Now let us suppose that the dream-pictures are what might be called the physiological delusion-products of a man, the compromise-results of that struggle between what is repressed and what is dominant that probably goes on in every person, even those absolutely normal in the daytime. Then we understand that we have to consider dream-images as something distorted behind which there is to be sought something else, not distorted, but, in a sense, something offensive, like Hanold's repressed memories behind his fantasies. We may express the contrast thus recognized by differentiating what the dreamer remembers on waking, the *manifest dream-content,* from what constituted the basis of the dream before the censor's distortion, the *latent dream-thoughts.* To interpret a dream, then, means to translate the manifest dream-content into the latent dream-thoughts, to undo the distortion which the latter had to suffer at the hands of the resistance censorship. If we bring these considerations to bear upon the dream occupying us, we find that the latent dream-thoughts must have been as follows: "The girl who has that beautiful walk you are seeking really lives in this city with you." But in this form the thought could not become conscious; in its way there stood the fact that a fantasy had established, as a result of a previous compromise, the idea that Gradiva was a Pompeiian girl. Therefore, if the actual fact of her living in the same locality and at the same time was to be preserved, there was nothing left to do but to make the distortion: "You are living in Pompeii at the time of Gradiva." And this, then, is the idea which the manifest dream-content makes real and represents as a present time which he is living in.

A dream is rarely the representation—one might say, the staging—of a single thought, but generally of a number of them, a web of thoughts. In Hanold's dream there is conspicuous another component of the content, whose distortion is easily removed so that one may learn the latent idea represented by it. This is a part of the dream to which the assurance of reality at the dream's end can also be extended. In the dream the beautiful walker, Gradiva, is transformed into a bas-relief. That is, of course, nothing but an in-

genious and poetic representation of the actual procedure.
Hanold had indeed transferred his interest from the living
girl to the bas-relief; the beloved had been transformed into
a stone relief. The latent dream-thoughts, which must remain unconscious, want to transform the relief back into the
living girl. In connection with the foregoing they say something like this to him: "You are interested in the bas-relief of
Gradiva only because it reminds you of the contemporary
Zoë who lives here." But this insight, if it could become conscious, would mean the end of the delusion.

Is it our duty to substitute unconscious thoughts for
every single bit of the manifest dream-content in such a
manner? Strictly speaking, yes; in the interpretation of a
dream which was actually dreamed we should not be allowed to shirk this duty. The dreamer would then have to
give us an exhaustive account. It is easily understood that
we cannot enforce such a demand in the case of an author's
creature; we will not, however, overlook the fact that we
have yet to submit the chief content of the dream to the
work of interpretation or translation.

Hanold's dream is, of course, an anxiety-dream. Its content is frightening; anxiety is felt by the dreamer in sleep,
and painful feelings remain after it. That is not of any great
help in our attempt at explanation; we are again forced to
borrow largely from the teachings of dream-interpretation.
This admonishes us not to make the mistake of deriving the
fear that is felt in a dream from its content, not to use the
content of a dream like the content of ideas in waking life.
It calls to our attention how often we dream the most horrible things without feeling any trace of fear. Rather, the
true state of affairs is a quite different one which cannot be

easily guessed, but can certainly be proved. The fear in the anxiety-dream corresponds to a sex-feeling, a libidinous emotion, like every neurotic fear, and has, through the process of repression, proceeded from the libido.[8] In the interpretation of dreams one must, therefore, substitute sexual excitement for fear. The fear which has thus come into existence now exercises—not regularly, but frequently—a selective influence on the dream-content and brings into the dream ideational elements which, in the conscious and erroneous conception of the dream, seem to be in keeping with this fear. This is, as has been said, by no means regularly the case, for there are anxiety-dreams in which the content is not at all frightful, in which, therefore, one cannot explain consciously the anxiety experienced.

I know that this explanation of fear in dreams sounds odd and is not easily believed; but I can only advise a friendly acceptance of it. It would, moreover, be rather peculiar if Norbert Hanold's dream allowed itself to be connected with this conception of fear and to be explained by it. We should then say that in the dreamer the erotic desire stirs at night, makes a powerful advance to bring his memory of the beloved into his consciousness and thus snatch him from the delusion, experiences another rejection and transformation into fear, which now, for its part, brings the fearful pictures from the academic memory of the dreamer into the dream-content. In this way the peculiar unconscious content of the dream, the amorous longing for the once-

[8] Cf. Freud, "Über die Berechtigung, von der Neurasthenie einen bestimmten Komplex als 'Angstneurose' abzutrennen" ("On the Justification for Detaching from Neurasthenia a Certain Complex Called 'Anxiety Neurosis'"), in *Sammlung kleiner Schriften zur Neurosenlehre* (1895). Cf. also *Traumdeutung*, first edition, p. 344 (*Interpretation of Dreams*, 1913 edition, p. 441).

known Zoë, is transformed into the manifest content of the destruction of Pompeii and the loss of Gradiva.

I believe this sounds quite plausible so far. One might justly argue that if erotic wishes constitute the undistorted content of this dream, then one must be able to point out, in the transformed dream, at least a recognizable remnant of these wishes hidden somewhere. Well, perhaps even this will come about with the aid of a suggestion which appears later in the story. At the first meeting with the supposed Gradiva, Hanold remembers this dream and requests the apparition to lie down again as he has seen her.[9] Thereupon the young lady rises, indignant, and leaves her strange companion in whose delusion-ridden speech she has heard the suggestion of an improper erotic wish. I think we may adopt Gradiva's interpretation; even of a real dream one cannot always demand more definiteness in the representation of an erotic wish.

Thus the application of some rules of dream-interpretation to Hanold's first dream has succeeded in making this dream comprehensible to us in its chief features and in fitting it into the sequence of the story. Then it must have been produced by its author with due consideration for these rules. One could raise only one more question: why the author should introduce a dream for further developing the delusion. Well, I think that is very cleverly arranged and again keeps faith with reality. We have already heard that in actual illness the formation of a delusion very often attaches to a dream, but after our explanation of the nature of dreams, we need find no new riddle in this fact. Dreams

[9] "No—not talked—but I called to you when you lay down to sleep and stood near you then—your face was as calmly beautiful as if it were of marble. May I beg you—rest it again on the step in that way."

and delusions spring from the same source, the repressed; the dream is, so to speak, the physiological delusion of the normal human being. Before the repressed has become strong enough to push itself up into waking life as a delusion, it may easily have won its first success under the more favorable conditions of sleep, in the form of a dream whose effect lingers on. During sleep, with the diminution of psychic activity, there occurs a slackening in the strength of the resistance which the dominant psychic forces offer the repressed material. This slackening is what makes dream-formation possible, and therefore the dream becomes, for us, the best avenue of approach to knowledge of the unconscious psyche. Only, the dream usually fades away rapidly with the re-establishment of the psychic content of waking life, and the ground gained by the unconscious is again evacuated.

## III

In the further course of the story there is another dream which can tempt us, perhaps even more than the first, to try to interpret it and fit it into the psychic life of the hero. But we save little if we leave the presentation of our author here in order to hasten directly to this second dream, for whoever wishes to interpret the dream of another cannot help concerning himself as extensively as possible with every subjective and objective experience of the dreamer. Therefore it would be best to keep to the thread of the story and provide it with our commentaries as we go along.

The new delusion about the death of Gradiva at the destruction of Pompeii in the year 79 is not the only aftereffect of the first dream we analyzed. Directly afterwards Hanold decides upon a trip to Italy, which finally takes him to Pompeii. Before this, however, something else has happened to him; leaning from his window, he thinks he sees on the street a figure with the bearing and walk of his Gradiva, hastens after her despite his scanty attire, does not overtake her, but is driven back by the jeers of the people on the street. After he has returned to his room, the song of a canary whose cage hangs in the window of the house across the street calls forth in him a mood such as if he wished to get from prison into freedom, and the spring trip is no sooner decided upon than it is accomplished.

Our author has put this trip of Hanold's in a specially strong light and has given our hero partial lucidity as to his subjective processes. Hanold has, of course, given himself a scientific pretext for his journey, but this is not substantial. He knows full well that the "impulse to travel has originated in a nameless feeling." A peculiar restlessness makes him dissatisfied with everything he encounters and drives him from Rome to Naples, from there to Pompeii, without his mood's being set right even at the last stopping-place. He is annoyed by the foolishness of honeymoon travelers and is enraged at the boldness of houseflies which populate the hotels of Pompeii; but finally he does not deceive himself over the fact that "his dissatisfaction was probably not caused by his surroundings alone, but to a degree had its origin in him." He considers himself overstrained, feels "that he was out of sorts because he lacked something without being able to explain what, and this ill-humor he took everywhere with him." In such a mood he is enraged even at his mistress, science; as he wanders through Pompeii for the first time in the glow of the midday sun, "not only had all his science left him, but it had left him without the least desire to regain it; he remembered it as from a great distance, and he felt that it had been like an old, dried-up, boring aunt, the dullest and most superfluous creature in the world."

In this unedifying and confused state of mind, one of the riddles connected with this journey is solved for him at the moment when he first sees Gradiva walking through Pompeii; he became conscious, for the first time, that "he had, without himself knowing the motive in his heart, come to Italy on that account, and had, without stop, continued from Rome and Naples to Pompeii to see if he could here find any trace of her (and that in a literal sense), for, with her unusual gait, she must have left behind in the ashes a footprint different from all the others."

As our author has put so much care into the delineation of this trip, it must be worth our while to explain its relation to Hanold's delusion and its place in the sequence of events. The journey is undertaken for motives which our hero does not at first recognize and does not admit to himself until later—motives which our author designates directly as "unconscious." This is certainly true to life; one does not need to have a delusion to act this way. It is rather an everyday occurrence, even in normal people, that they are deceived about the motives of their actions and do not become conscious of them until afterward, when a conflict of several emotional currents establishes for them the causality of such confusion. Hanold's trip, therefore, was intended, from the beginning, to serve the delusion and was to take him to Pompeii to continue there the search for Gradiva. Let us remember that before and directly after the dream this search filled his mind and that the dream itself was only an

answer, stifled by his consciousness, to the question about
the whereabouts of Gradiva. However, some force which
we do not recognize prevents the delusional plan from becoming conscious, for the time being, so that only inadequate
pretexts, which must be renewed periodically, are available
for the conscious motivation of the trip. The author gives
us another riddle by having the dream, the discovery of the
supposed Gradiva on the street, and the decision to make
the journey because of the influence of the singing canary
follow one another like random occurrences without inner
coherence.

With the help of the explanations which we derive from
the later speeches of Zoë Bertgang, this obscure part of the
tale is illumined for our understanding. It was really the
original of Gradiva, Miss Zoë herself, whom Hanold saw
from his window walking on the street and whom he would
soon have overtaken. The message of the dream—"she is
really living now in the present, in the same city with you"
—would thus, by a lucky chance, have received an irrefutable corroboration, before which his inner resistance would
have collapsed. The canary, however, whose song impelled
Hanold to go away, belonged to Zoë, and its cage was in her
window, in the house diagonally across from Hanold's.
Hanold, who, according to the girl's accusation, was endowed with "negative hallucination" and mastered the art
of not seeing or recognizing even living people, must from
the beginning have had unconscious knowledge of what we
do not discover until later. The signs of Zoë's proximity, her
appearance on the street, and her bird's song so near his
window intensify the effect of the dream, and in this condition, so dangerous for his resistance to eroticism, he takes

flight. His journey arises from the recovery of the resistance after that advance of erotic desire in the dream; it is an attempt at flight from the living and present beloved. In practical terms, it means a victory for repression, which this time keeps the upper hand in the delusion, whereas in his former action, the "pedestrian investigations" of women and girls, the eroticism had been victorious. However, in this indecision of the struggle, the compromise nature of the results is maintained everywhere; the trip to Pompeii, which is to take him away from the living Zoë, leads to her substitute, Gradiva. The journey which is undertaken in defiance of the latent dream-thoughts does follow the instructions of the manifest dream-content to go to Pompeii. Thus delusion triumphs anew every time that eroticism and resistance struggle anew.

This conception of Hanold's trip as a flight from the awakening erotic desire for the beloved who is so near harmonizes, however, with the frame of mind portrayed in him during his stay in Italy. The rejection of eroticism, which dominates him, expresses itself there in his abhorrence of honeymoon travelers. A little dream in the *albergo* in Rome, caused by the proximity of a couple of German lovers, "Augustus" and "Gretchen," whose evening conversation he is forced to overhear through the thin partition, casts further light on the erotic tendencies of his first great dream. The new dream transports him again to Pompeii, where Vesuvius is just having another eruption, and thus refers to the dream which continues active during his trip. But among the imperiled people he sees this time, not, as before, himself and Gradiva, but Apollo Belvedere and the Capitoline Venus—doubtless an ironic exaltation of the couple in the adjoining room. Apollo lifts Venus, carries her away, and places her on an object in the dark which seems to be a carriage or a cart, for a "rattling sound" comes from it. Otherwise the dream requires no special skill for its interpretation.

Our author, whom we have long relied upon not to make a single stroke in his picture idly and without purpose, has given us another bit of testimony for the non-sexual force dominating Hanold on the trip. During his hours of wandering about Pompeii, it happens that, "strangely enough, he did not even once remember that he had dreamed some time ago that he had been present at the destruction of Pompeii by the volcanic eruption of 79." Only at the sight of Gradiva does he suddenly remember this dream, and at the same time he becomes conscious of the delusional motive for his puzzling journey. What other meaning could there be for this forgetting of the dream, for this repression-boundary between the dream and the psychic condition on the journey, than that the journey is the result not of the direct instigation of the dream, but of a rebellion against this latter, as an emanation from a psychic force which does not want to know about the secret meaning of the dream?

On the other hand, Hanold is not happy about this victory over his eroticism. The suppressed psychic impulse remains strong enough to revenge itself, through discomfort and frustration, on the suppressing agency. His longing has changed to restlessness and dissatisfaction, which make the trip seem senseless to him. His insight into the motivation of his trip in the service of the delusion is obstructed; his relationship to science, which ought to stir all his interest in such a place, is upset. So our author shows his hero, after his flight from love, in a sort of crisis, in an utterly confused and unsettled condition, in a derangement such as usually appears at the climax of illness if neither of the two struggling forces is so much stronger than the other that the difference could establish a strict psychic regime. Here our author takes hold to help and to settle; for, at this point, he introduces Gradiva, who undertakes the cure of the delusion. With his power to direct to a happy solution the fortunes of all the characters created by him, in spite of all the requirements which he makes them conform to, he transports the girl from whom Hanold has fled to Pompeii to that very place, thus correcting the folly which the delusion caused the young man to commit in leaving the home town of his beloved for the burial-place of the one substituted for her by his fantasy.

With the appearance of Zoë Bertgang as Gradiva, which marks the climax in the suspense of the story, our interest is soon diverted. If we have hitherto been living through the development of a delusion, we are now to become witnesses of its cure, and may ask ourselves if our author has merely invented the procedure of this cure or has carried it out according to actually existing possibilities. From Zoë's own words in the conversation with her friend, we have decidedly the right to ascribe to her an intention to cure the hero. But how does she go about it? After she has suppressed the indignation aroused in her by his presumptuous request to lie down to sleep again, as "then," she appears again the next day at the same place and elicits from Hanold all the secret knowledge that she lacked for an understanding of his conduct of the previous day. She learns of his dream, of the bas-relief of Gradiva, and of the peculiarity of walk which she shares with the relief. She accepts the role of a spirit awakened to life for a brief hour, which, she observes, his delusion assigns to her, and in ambiguous words she gently gives him a new role by accepting from him the grave-flower which he had brought along without conscious purpose, and expresses regret that he has not given her roses.

Our interest in the conduct of this eminently clever girl, who has decided to win the lover of her youth as husband after she has recognized his love as the impelling force behind his delusion, is, however, restrained at this place, probably by the strange feelings that the delusion can arouse even in us. Its latest development, that Gradiva, who was buried in the year 79, can now exchange conversation with him as a noon-spirit for an hour, after the passing of which she sinks out of sight or seeks her grave again—this chimera, which is not confused by the sight of her modern footgear, nor by her ignorance of the ancient tongues, nor by her command of German, which did not exist in those times, seems indeed to justify the author's designation, "A Pompeiian Fancy," but to exclude every standard of clinical reality. And yet on closer consideration the improbability in this delusion seems to me to vanish for the most part. To be sure, our author has taken upon himself a part of the blame, and in the first part of the story he has offered the fact that Zoë was the image of the bas-relief in every detail. One must therefore guard against transferring this improbability from this premise to its corollary, namely, that Hanold considers the girl to be Gradiva come to life. The value of the delusional explanation is increased by the fact that the author has placed no rational one at our disposal.

In the glowing sun of the Campagna and in the bewildering magic powers of the vine which grows on Vesuvius, our author has introduced other factors which serve to explain and mitigate the hero's transgression.

But the most important of all explanatory and exonerating considerations remains the facility with which our intellect decides to accept an absurd content if impulses with a strong emotional stress find their satisfaction thereby. It is astonishing (and this generally meets with too little acceptance) how easily and frequently intelligent people give reactions of partial feeble-mindedness under such psychological constellations; anyone who is not too conceited may observe this in himself as often as he wishes, and especially when some of the thought-processes concerned are connected with unconscious or repressed motives. I cite in this connection the words of a philosopher who writes to me: "I have also begun to make note of cases of striking mistakes, from my own experience, of thoughtless actions which one subsequently explains to himself (in a very unreasonable way). It is frightening but characteristic how much stupidity comes to light in this way."

Now let us add the fact that belief in spirits, apparitions, and returning souls (which gets so much support in the religions to which, at least as children, all of us have clung) is by no means destroyed among all educated people and that many otherwise sensible people find their interest in spiritism compatible with their reason. Indeed, even one become dispassionate and skeptical may perceive with shame how easily he turns back for a moment to a belief in spirits, when emotion and perplexity concur in him. I know of a physician who had once lost a patient by Basedow's

disease and could not rid himself of the slight suspicion
that he had perhaps contributed to the unfortunate outcome
by unwise medication. One day several years later there
came into his office a girl in whom, despite all reluctance,
he was obliged to recognize the dead woman. His only
thought was that it was true that the dead can return, and
his fear did not give way to shame until the visitor introduced herself as the sister of the woman who had died of
Basedow's disease. This disease lends to those afflicted with
it a great similarity of features, something that can often be
noticed, and in this case this characteristic resemblance was
superimposed upon the family resemblance. Incidentally,
the physician to whom this happened was myself, and for
this reason I should hardly be inclined to quarrel with
Norbert Hanold over the clinical possibility of his short
delusion about Gradiva having returned to life. Finally, it
is well known to every psychiatrist that in serious cases of
chronic delusion (paranoia), the most extreme absurdities,
ingeniously elaborated and well presented, may be observed.

After his first meeting with Gradiva, Norbert Hanold had
drunk his wine in first one and then the other of the hotels
in Pompeii that were known to him, while the other guests
were having their regular meals. "Of course, in no way had
the absurd supposition entered his mind" that he was doing
this to find out in what hotel Gradiva lived and dined; but
it is hard to say what other significance his action could
have had. On the day after the second meeting in the house
of Meleager, he has all sorts of strange and apparently dis-
connected experiences: he finds a narrow cleft in the wall
of the portico where Gradiva had disappeared; meets a
foolish lizard-catcher who addresses him like an acquain-

tance; discovers a third, secluded hotel, the "Albergo del Sole," whose owner talks him into buying a metal brooch encrusted with green patina, which had been found with the remains of a Pompeiian girl; and finally notices in his own hotel a newly arrived young couple whom he diagnoses as brother and sister and finds congenial.

All these impressions are then woven into a "strangely nonsensical" dream, as follows: "Somewhere in the sun Gradiva sat making a trap out of a blade of grass, in order to catch a lizard, and she said: 'Please stay quite still—my colleague is right; the method is really good, and she has used it with the greatest success!' "

To this dream he offers resistance even while sleeping, with the criticism that it is indeed utter madness, and he tosses and turns in order to free himself from it. He succeeds in doing this, too, with the aid of an invisible bird who utters a short, merry call and carries the lizard away in its beak.

Shall we risk an attempt to interpret this dream also—that is, to substitute for it the latent thoughts from whose distortion it must have proceeded? It is as nonsensical as one could expect only a dream to be, and this absurdity of dreams is the mainstay of the view which denies to a dream the character of a valid psychic act and considers that it proceeds from a desultory stimulus of psychic elements.

We can apply to this dream the technique which can be designated as the regular procedure of dream-interpretation. It consists in disregarding the apparent sequence in the manifest dream, but in examining separately every part of the content and in seeking its derivation in the impressions, memories, and free associations of the dreamer. Since we cannot examine Hanold, however, we must be satisfied with making reference to his impressions and may, but only quite modestly, substitute our own ideas for his.

"Somewhere in the sun Gradiva sat catching lizards, and said . . ." What impression of the day is this part of the dream reminiscent of? Unquestionably of the meeting with the elderly gentleman, the lizard-catcher, for whom Gradiva is substituted in the dream. He was sitting or lying on a "hot, sunny" slope and spoke to Hanold, too. Even Gradiva's utterances in the dream are copied from those of the man. Let us compare: "'The method suggested by my colleague, Eimer, is really good; I have already used it often with the best of success. Please keep quite still.'" Gradiva speaks quite similarly in the dream, except that for the "colleague, Eimer," there is substituted an unnamed woman colleague; the *often* in the zoologist's speech is missing in the dream; and the order of the sentences has been changed somewhat. It seems, therefore, that this experience of the day has been transformed into a dream by certain changes and distortions. Why did this happen, and what is the meaning of the distortions—the substitution of Gradiva for the old gentleman and the introduction of the puzzling "woman colleague"?

There is a rule of dream-interpretation which says: A speech heard in a dream always originates from a speech either heard or uttered in waking life. Well, this rule seems followed here; Gradiva's speech is only a modification of a speech heard in the daytime from the old zoologist. Another rule of dream-interpretation would tell us that the substitution of one person for another, or the mixture of two people (e.g., by showing one in a position which is characteristic of another), means the equating of the two people, a cor-

respondence between them. Let us venture to apply this
rule also to our dream. Then the interpretation would be
as follows: "Gradiva catches lizards, as that old gentleman
does, and, like him, is skilled in lizard-catching." This result
is not comprehensible yet, but we still have another riddle
before us. To which impression of the day shall we refer the
"woman colleague" who is substituted in the dream for the
famous zoologist, Eimer? Fortunately we have not much
choice here; only one other girl can be meant by "woman
colleague," the congenial young lady in whom Hanold has
conjectured a sister traveling with her brother. "On her
gown she wore a red Sorrento rose, the sight of which, as
he looked across from the corner, stirred something in his
memory without his being able to think what it was." This
observation on the part of the author surely gives us the
right to assert that she is the "woman colleague" of the
dream. What Hanold cannot remember is certainly nothing
else than the remark of the supposed Gradiva, as she asked
him for the grave-flower, that to more fortunate girls one
brought roses in spring. In this speech, however, lay a
hidden wooing. What kind of lizard-catching is it that this
more fortunate woman colleague has been so successful
with?

On the next day Hanold surprises the supposed brother
and sister in a tender embrace and can thus correct his
mistake of the previous day. They are really a couple of
lovers, on their honeymoon, as we learn later when the two
so unexpectedly disturb Hanold's third meeting with Zoë.
If we will now accept the idea that Hanold, who consciously
considers them brother and sister, has unconsciously recognized at once their real relationship, which on the next day

reveals itself so unequivocally, there results a good meaning for Gradiva's remark in the dream. The red rose then becomes a symbol for being in love; Hanold understands that the two are as Gradiva and he are yet to be. The lizard-catching acquires the meaning of husband-catching, and Gradiva's speech means something like this: "Let me arrange things; I know how to win a husband as well as this other girl does."

Why must this insight into Zoë's intentions appear in the dream in the form of the speech of the old zoologist? Why is Zoë's skill in husband-catching represented by the old man's skill in lizard-catching? Well, it is easy for us to answer that question; we have long since guessed that the lizard-catcher is none other than the professor of Zoology, Bertgang, Zoë's father, who must of course also know Hanold, so that he addresses him as an acquaintance as a matter of course. Again, let us accept the idea that Hanold, in his unconscious, immediately recognizes the professor: "It seemed to him dimly that he had already seen the face of the lizard-hunter, probably in one of the two hotels." Thus is explained the strange cloaking of the purpose attributed to Zoë. She is the daughter of the lizard-catcher; she has inherited this skill from him. The substitution of Gradiva for the lizard-catcher in the dream-content is thus the representation of the relation between the two people, which was recognized by the unconscious; the introduction of "woman colleague" in place of "colleague, Eimer" allows the dream to express comprehension of her courtship of the man. The dream has so far welded two of the day's experiences into one situation, "condensed" them, as we say, in order to procure what is, to be sure, a rather unrecognizable expression for two ideas which are not allowed to become conscious. But we can go on to diminish the strangeness of the dream still more and to point out the influence of other experiences of the day on the formation of the manifest dream.

We might express our dissatisfaction with the foregoing explanation as to why the scene of the lizard-catching, of all things, was made the nucleus of the dream, and suppose that still other elements in the dream-thoughts exerted their influence in behalf of the honoring of the "lizard" in the manifest dream. This could quite easily be the case. Let us recall that Hanold has discovered a cleft in the wall, in the place where Gradiva seems to him to disappear; this is "wide enough to afford passage to an unusually slender figure." By this perception he is forced in the daytime to make a revision in his delusion: Gradiva did not sink into the ground when she disappeared from his sight, but was going back, by this route, to her grave. In his unconscious thought he might say to himself that he had now found the natural explanation for the surprising disappearance of the girl; but must not forcing one's self through narrow clefts and disappearing into them recall the conduct of lizards? Does not Gradiva herself, in this connection, behave like an agile little lizard? We think, therefore, that the discovery of this cleft in the wall had acted as a determinant on the choice of the "lizard" element for the manifest dream-content; the lizard-situation of the dream thus represented this impression of the day as well as the meeting with the zoologist, Zoë's father.

What if we were sufficiently emboldened now to attempt to find in the dream-content a representation also of the one experience of the day which has not yet been turned to account, the discovery of the third hotel, "del Sole"? Our author has treated this episode so exhaustively and linked so much with it that we should be surprised if it alone had made no contribution to the dream-formation. Hanold enters this hotel which, because of its secluded location and its distance from the station, has remained unknown to him, to get a bottle of limewater for congestion of the blood. The hotelkeeper takes this opportunity to extol his antiques and shows him a brooch which, it was alleged, had belonged to that Pompeiian girl who was found near the Forum in fond embrace with her lover. Hanold, who had never before believed this frequently repeated story, is now compelled, by a force unknown to him, to believe in the truth of this touching story and in the genuineness of the article found. He buys the brooch and leaves the hotel with his purchase. In passing, he sees nodding down at him from one of the windows a cluster of white asphodel-blossoms which had been placed in a water glass, and he feels that this sight is an attestation of the genuineness of his new possession. The sincere conviction is now impressed upon him that the green brooch belonged to Gradiva and that she was the girl who died in her lover's embrace. The tormenting jealousy which thereupon seizes him he appeases with the resolution to assure himself about this suspicion the next day from Gradiva herself by showing her the brooch. This is certainly a strange bit of new delusion. Should not a trace point to it in the dream of the following night?

It will be well worth our while to get an understanding of the origin of this addition to the delusion, to look up the new bit of unconscious insight for which the new bit of delusion is substituted. The delusion originates under the influence of the proprietor of the Sun Hotel, toward whom Hanold conducts himself in such a strangely gullible manner, as if he were under his suggestion. The proprietor shows him a small metal brooch as genuine and as the possession of that girl who was found in the arms of her lover, buried in the ashes. Hanold, who could be critical enough to doubt the veracity of the story as well as the genuineness of the brooch, is immediately caught, credulous, and buys the more-than-doubtful antique. It is quite incomprehensible why he should act this way, and no hint is given that the personality of the proprietor himself might solve this riddle for us. There is, however, another riddle in this incident, and two riddles sometimes solve each other. On leaving the *albergo,* our hero catches sight of an asphodel cluster in a glass at a window, and takes this as evidence that the metal brooch is genuine. How can that be? This last point is fortunately easy of solution. The white flower is probably the one he presented to Gradiva at noon, and it is quite correct that through the sight of it at one of the windows of this hotel something is corroborated—not the genuineness of the brooch, to be sure, but something else which has become clear to him at the discovery of this formerly overlooked *albergo.* On the previous day he already acted as if he were trying to find out, in the two Pompeii hotels, where the person lived who appeared to him as Gradiva. Now, as he stumbles so unexpectedly upon a third hotel, he must be saying to himself in the unconscious, "So she lives here." And then, on leaving, "Oh, yes, here is the asphodel flower I gave her; then that is her window." This, then, is the new idea for which the delusion is substituted and which cannot become conscious because its premise that Gradiva is living, a person he once knew, was not able to become conscious.

But how is the substitution of the delusion for the new insight supposed to have occurred? In this way, I think: that the feeling of conviction which attached to the insight was able to assert itself and persisted, while the insight incapable of consciousness was replaced by a different ideational content, but one bound up with it through thought-connection. Thus the feeling of conviction was connected with a content actually alien to it, and this latter attained, as delusion, a recognition which was not due it. Hanold transfers his conviction that Gradiva lives in this house to other impressions which he receives in the house; in this way he becomes credulous about what the proprietor says, the genuineness of the metal brooch, and the truth of the anecdote about the lovers found in an embrace, but only in the sense that he connects what he has heard in this house with Gradiva. The jealousy which has been in readiness in him takes hold of this material, and there arises the delusion, even in contradiction to his first dream, that Gradiva was the girl who died in the arms of her lover and that the brooch which he bought belonged to her.

We notice that the conversation with Gradiva and her gentle "flowery" [1] wooing have already produced important changes in Hanold. Traits of male desire, components of the libido, are awakened in him—although, to be sure, they cannot yet dispense with concealment through conscious pretexts. But the problem of the "corporeal nature" of Gradiva, which has pursued him all day, cannot disavow its derivation from a young man's erotic curiosity about the female

---

[1] [Freud's pun is *durch die Blume:* literally "through the flower," figuratively "subtle," "subtly," or "allusively."—TRANS.]

body, even if it is to be shifted to the scientific sphere by deliberate emphasis on Gradiva's peculiar hovering between life and death. Jealousy is an additional sign of Hanold's awakening activity in love; he expresses this jealousy at the opening of the conversation on the next day, and with the aid of a new pretext achieves his object of touching the girl's body and of striking her, as in times long past.

Now, however, it is time to ask if the course of delusion-formation which we have inferred from our author's representation is one known from other instances or one even possible. From our medical experience, we can answer only that it is surely the right way, perhaps the only one, in which the delusion attains the unshakeable acceptance which is part of its clinical character. If the patient believes so firmly in his delusion, this does not happen because of an inversion of his powers of judgment and does not proceed from what is erroneous in the delusion. Rather, in every delusion there is also a little grain of truth; there is something in it which really deserves belief, and this is the source of the conviction of the patient, who is to this extent justified. This true element, however, has been repressed for a long time; if it finally succeeds in penetrating into consciousness (this time in distorted form), the feeling of conviction attached to it is overly strong, as if by way of compensation, and now it clings to the distortion-substitute of the repressed true element and guards it against any critical impugnment. The conviction shifts, as it were, from the unconscious, true element to the conscious, erroneous one connected with it, and remains fixed there as a result of this very displacement. The case of delusion-formation which resulted from Hanold's first dream is nothing but a similar, even though not identical, case of such a displacement. Indeed, the depicted manner in which conviction develops in a delusion is not even fundamentally different from the way in which conviction is formed in normal cases, where repression is not involved. All of us attach our convictions to thought-contents in which the true and the false are combined, and let these convictions reach out from the former and extend to the latter. They spread out, as it were, from the true over the false that is associated with it and protect the false against deserved criticism, even if not so immutably as in a delusion. Connections—"pull," so to speak—can serve as substitutes for intrinsic merit in normal psychology, too.

I will now return to the dream and single out a small but not uninteresting feature which establishes a connection between two occasions of the dream. Gradiva had established a certain contrast between the white asphodel flower and the red rose. Finding the asphodel flower again in the window of the "Albergo del Sole" becomes a weighty proof for Hanold's unconscious insight which expresses itself in a new delusion; and to this is added the fact that the red rose on the dress of the congenial young girl helps Hanold, in the unconscious, to attain the correct view of her relationship to her companion, so that he can have her appear in his dream as a "woman colleague."

But where in the manifest dream-content is there found the trace and representation of that discovery of Hanold's which we found replaced by the new delusion—the discovery that Gradiva is living with her father in that third, out-of-the-way hotel in Pompeii, the "Albergo del Sole"? Well, it is in the dream in its entirety and not even in very distorted form. But I hesitate to point it out, for I know that, even with readers whose patience with me has lasted this long, a strong opposition to my attempts at interpretation will be stirred up. Hanold's discovery is given in full in the dream-content, I repeat, but so cleverly concealed that one must needs overlook it. It is hidden there behind a play on words, an ambiguity. "Somewhere in the sun Gradiva sat"; this we have rightly connected with the locality where Hanold met the zoologist, her father. But can it not also mean "in the Sun"—that is, Gradiva lives in the "Albergo del Sole," in the Sun Hotel? And doesn't the "somewhere," which has no reference to the meeting with her father, sound so hypocritically indefinite precisely because it introduces the definite information about Gradiva's whereabouts? From previous experience in the interpretation of real dreams I am quite certain of such a meaning in the ambiguity, but I should really not venture to offer this bit of interpretation to my readers if our author did not lend me his powerful assistance here. On the next day he puts into the mouth of the girl, when she sees the metal brooch, the same pun which we accept for the interpretation of that spot in the dream-content. "Did you find it in the Sun, perhaps? . . . *Die macht hier solche Kunststücke.*" [2] And when Hanold does not understand this remark, she explains that she means the Sun Hotel, which is called "Sole" here and from where the supposed antique is also familiar to her.

And now we should like to make the attempt to substitute for Hanold's "strangely nonsensical" dream unconscious

[2] [The pun in the latter part of her statement might be translated: "It performs such tricks around here." *Kunststück* commonly means "feat," "trick," or "stunt." But because the word is compounded of *Kunst* (art) and *Stück* (piece), the statement could also imply that the Sun Hotel specializes in producing fake *objets d'art.*—TRANS.]

thoughts hidden behind it, and quite unlike it. They run
somewhat as follows: "She lives in the Sun with her father;
why is she playing such a game with me? Does she wish to
make fun of me? Or could it be possible that she loves me
and wishes for a husband?" To this latter possibility there
now follows in sleep the rejection—"This is utter madness"
—which is apparently directed against the entire manifest
dream.

Critical readers now have the right to inquire about the
origin of that interpolation, hitherto not substantiated,
which refers to being made fun of by Gradiva. To this, *The
Interpretation of Dreams* gives the answer; if taunts and
sneers or embittered opposition occur in dream-thoughts,
they are expressed by the nonsensical course of the manifest
dream, through the absurdity in the dream. The latter
means, therefore, no paralysis of psychic activity, but is one
of the means of representation which the dream-work utilizes. As always in especially difficult passages, our author
comes to our assistance here. The nonsensical dream has a
brief postlude in which a bird utters a merry call and takes
away the lizard in his beak. Such a laughing call Hanold
had heard after Gradiva's disappearance. It actually came
from Zoë, who was shaking off the melancholy seriousness
of her underworld role; with this laugh Gradiva had really
derided him. The dream-image, however, of the bird carrying away the lizard may recall that other one in a previous
dream in which Apollo Belvedere carried away the Capitoline Venus.

Perhaps some readers are still under the impression that
the translation of the lizard-catching situation into the idea
of wooing is not sufficiently justified. Additional support

may be found in the hint that Zoë, in conversation with her colleague, admits about herself the very thing that Hanold's thoughts suppose about her, when she says that she had been sure of "digging up" something interesting for herself here in Pompeii. She thereby delves into the archaeological sphere of ideas, as he did into the zoological with his allegory of lizard-catching, as if they were striving to approach each other and each wished to assume the characteristics of the other.

Thus we have finished the interpretation of the second dream. Both have become accessible to our understanding under the presupposition that the dreamer, in his unconscious thought, knows all that he has forgotten in his conscious, that in the former he correctly appraises everything that he delusively misconstrues in the latter. In our interpretations we have, of course, been obliged to make many an assertion that sounded odd to the reader because it was strange to him and probably often aroused the suspicion that we were claiming as our author's meaning what is only our own. We are ready to do everything to dissipate this suspicion, and will therefore gladly consider more exhaustively one of the most ticklish points—I mean the use of ambiguous words and speeches as in the example, "Somewhere in the sun (*or Sun*) Gradiva sat."

It must strike the attention of every reader of *Gradiva* how often our author puts into the mouths of the two leading characters speeches that have double meaning. For Hanold these speeches are intended to have only one meaning, and only his companion, Gradiva, is affected by their other meaning. Thus, after her first answer, he exclaims: "I knew that your voice would sound like that"; and the as yet

unenlightened Zoë has to ask how that is possible, as he has
never before heard her speak. In the second conversation,
the girl doubts his delusion for a moment when he assures
her that he has recognized her at once. She must understand these words in the meaning that is correct for his
unconscious, as his recognition of their acquaintance which
reaches back into childhood, while he, of course, knows
nothing of this meaning of his speech and explains it only
by reference to the delusion which dominates him. On the
other hand, the speeches of the girl—in whose person the
most brilliant mental clarity is opposed to the delusion—
are intentionally made ambiguous. One meaning of them
falls in with the ideas of Hanold's delusion, in order to
enable her to penetrate into his conscious comprehension;
the other raises itself above the delusion and, as a rule, gives
us its translation into the unconscious truth represented by
it. It is a triumph of wit to be able to represent the delusion
and the truth in one and the same mode of expression.

Interspersed with such ambiguities is Zoë's speech in
which she explains the situation to her woman friend and
at the same time gets rid of her disturbing company; it is
really spoken out of the book, calculated more for us readers
than for her happy colleague. In the conversations with
Hanold, the double meaning is established mostly through
Zoë's use of the symbolism which we find followed in
Hanold's first dream, in the equation of burial and repression,
Pompeii and childhood. Thus on the one hand she can, in
her speeches, continue in the role which Hanold's delusion
assigns to her; on the other, she can touch upon the real
relations and awaken in his unconscious an understanding
of them.

"I have long accustomed myself to being dead." "For me, the flower of oblivion is the right one from your hand." In these speeches there is a gentle hint of the reproof which then breaks out clearly enough in her last sermon when she compares him to an archaeopteryx. "To think that a person must first die to become alive; but for archaeologists that is necessary, I suppose," she says later, after the solution of the delusion, as if to give us the key to her ambiguous speeches. The most beautiful application of her symbolism appears, however, in this question: "It seems to me as if we had eaten our bread together like this once, two thousand years ago. Can't you remember it?" In this speech the substitution of historic antiquity for childhood and the effort to awaken his memory of the latter are quite unmistakable.

Whence, then, comes this obvious preference for ambiguous speeches in *Gradiva*? It seems to us not chance, but a necessary corollary of the premises of the tale. It is nothing but the counterpart of the twofold determination of symptoms, in so far as the speeches are themselves symptoms and, like these, proceed from compromises between the conscious and the unconscious. But one notices this double origin in the speeches more easily than in the actions; and when, as the flexibility of the material of the conversation often makes possible, each of the two intentions of a speech succeeds in expressing itself through the same arrangement of words, then there is present what we call an "ambiguity."

During the psychotherapeutic treatment of a delusion or an analogous disturbance, one often brings out such ambiguous speeches in patients as new symptoms of a very transient nature, and can, on occasion, even make use of them oneself; not infrequently one can stimulate, with the

meaning intended for the patient's consciousness, his understanding for the meaning valid in his unconscious. I know
from experience that among the uninitiated this role of ambiguity usually gives the greatest offense and causes the
grossest misunderstandings; but our author was right, at
any rate, in representing in his production this characteristic
feature of the processes of the formation of dream and
delusion.

## IV

With Zoë's function as physician there is awakened in us
a new interest, as we have said. We are eager to learn if
such a cure as she accomplishes with Hanold is comprehensible or even possible, whether our author has observed
the conditions for the passing of a delusion as correctly as
he has those for its development.

Undoubtedly we shall here encounter a point of view
which denies the case portrayed by our author such a basic
interest and recognizes no problem requiring an explanation.
There is nothing left for Hanold to do, it may be argued, but
to resolve his delusion again, after its object, the supposed
Gradiva herself, convicts him of the incorrectness of all his
assertions and gives him the most natural explanations for
everything puzzling—for example, how she knows his name.
Thereby the affair would be settled logically. However, as
the girl has confessed her love to him in this connection,
our author surely would, for the satisfaction of his feminine
readers, let the otherwise not uninteresting story have the
usual happy ending—marriage. More consistent, and just
as possible, would have been the different conclusion that
the young scholar, after the explanation of his error, should,

with polite thanks, take his leave of the young lady and motivate his rejection of her love by saying that he might show an intensive interest in antique women of bronze and stone—or their originals if these were available—but that he had no use for a contemporary girl of flesh and blood. The archaeological fantasy, so it might be argued, was rather capriciously cemented together with a love story by our author.

In rejecting this conception as impossible, our attention is drawn to the fact that we have to attribute the change beginning in Norbert Hanold not to the relinquishment of the delusion alone. Together with—indeed, even before— the breaking up of the latter, there is in him an unmistakable awakening of the need for love, which then naturally results in his asking for the hand of the girl who has freed him from delusion. We have already shown under what pretexts and cloaks his curiosity about her corporeal nature, his jealousy, and the brutal male impulse for possession have been expressed in him in the midst of the delusion, ever since repressed desire has put the first dream into his mind. Let us add the further testimony that in the evening after the second talk with Gradiva, a living woman for the first time seems congenial to him, although he still makes a concession to his abhorrence of honeymoon travelers by not recognizing the likable girl as newly married. The next forenoon, however, chance makes him witness of an ex-change of caresses between the girl and her supposed brother, and he draws back shyly, as if he had disturbed a sacred rite. Disdain for "Augustus" and "Gretchen" is for-gotten, and respect for the erotic life is restored to him.

Thus our author has connected the breaking up of the

delusion and the breaking forth of the need for love most closely with each other and prepared the outcome in a love affair as necessary. He simply knows the nature of the delusion better than his critics; he knows that a component of amorous longing has combined with a component of resistance to form a delusion, and he lets the girl who undertakes the cure sense in Hanold's delusion the component agreeable to her. Only this insight can make her decide to devote herself to treating him; only the certainty of knowing herself loved by him can move her to confess her love to him. The treatment consists in restoring to him, from without, the repressed memories which he cannot release from within. It would be ineffective, however, if the therapist did not consider the emotions and if the interpretation of the delusion were not finally: "Look, all this means only that you love me."

The procedure which our author has his Zoë follow for the cure of the delusion of the friend of her youth shows, in its nature, a considerable resemblance to—indeed, a complete agreement with—a therapeutic method which Dr. J. Breuer and the present writer introduced into medicine in 1895 and to the perfection of which the latter has since devoted himself. This method of treatment, which Breuer first called the "cathartic," but which the present writer has preferred to designate as "analytic," consists in forcibly bringing into the consciousness of patients suffering from disturbances analogous to Hanold's delusion the unconscious, through the repression of which they have become ill, just as Gradiva does with the repressed memories of their childhood relations. To be sure, accomplishment of this task is easier for Gradiva than it is for the physician; she is, in this respect, in a position that might be considered ideal from many viewpoints. The physician who does not fathom his patient in advance and does not possess within himself, as conscious memory, what is working in the patient as unconscious, must enlist the aid of a complicated technique in order to overcome this disadvantage. He must learn to infer with absolute certainty, from the patient's conscious ideas and statements, the repressed material in him—to guess the unconscious when it betrays itself behind the patient's conscious expressions and acts. The physician then does something similar to what Norbert Hanold does by himself at the end of the story, when he retranslates the name "Gradiva" into *Bertgang*. The disturbance then disappears while it is being traced back to its origin; analysis brings the cure at the same time.

The similarity between Gradiva's procedure and the analytic method of psychotherapy is, however, not limited to these two points, making the repressed conscious and the concurrence of explanation and cure. It extends also to what proves to be the essential feature of the whole change—the awakening of the emotions. Every disturbance analogous to Hanold's delusion, which in science we usually designate as a psychoneurosis, has, as a preliminary, the repression of part of the emotional life—let us say confidently, of the sex-impulse. And at every attempt to introduce the unconscious and repressed cause of the illness into consciousness, the emotional component concerned necessarily awakens to renewed struggle with the forces repressing it, to achieve some adjustment with them in the end, often with violent manifestations of reaction. In a reawakening, in consciousness, of repressed love, the process of recovery is accomplished when we sum up all the various components of the sex-impulse as "love," and this reawakening is irremissible. For the symptoms on account of which the treatment was undertaken are nothing but the precipitation of former struggles of repression and recurrence and can be resolved and washed away only by a new high tide of these very passions. Every psychoanalytic treatment is an attempt to free repressed love, which has found a poor compromise-outlet in a symptom. Indeed, the conformity with the therapeutic process pictured by the author in *Gradiva* reaches a new high when we add that even in analytical psychotherapy the reawakened passion, whether love or hate, chooses the person of the physician as its object every time.

Then, to be sure, there appear the differences which make the case of Gradiva an ideal one such as medical skill cannot attain. Gradiva can requite the love which is pushing through from the unconscious into the conscious; the physician cannot. Gradiva was herself the object of the former repressed love; her person offers at once a desirable object to the freed erotic activity. The physician has been a stranger, and after the cure he must try to become a stranger again; often he is incapable of advising the cured patient as to how to apply in life his or her regained capacity for love. To suggest what resources and makeshifts the physician then employs to approach with more or less success the model of a love-cure which our author has drawn for us would carry us too far afield from our present task.

Now, however, we came to the last question that we have already evaded several times. Our views about repression, the formation of a delusion and related disturbances, the formation and breaking up of dreams, the role of the erotic life, and the manner of cure for such disturbances—these can by no means be regarded as the common property of science, let alone the easily obtained possession of educated people. If the insight which enables our author to create his *Fancy* in such a way that we can analyze it like a real history of disease is based on the above-mentioned knowledge, we should like to find out the source of it. A member of the circle which, as was explained at the beginning, was interested in the dreams of *Gradiva* and their possible interpretation, put the direct question to Wilhelm Jensen as to whether he had any knowledge of the scientific theories that are so similar to what is in his work. Our author answered, as was to be expected, in the negative and even somewhat testily. His imagination had inspired the *Gradiva*, who had given him pleasure; anyone whom she did not please might leave her alone. He did not suspect how much she had pleased the readers.

It is quite possible that our author's rejection does not stop at that. Perhaps he denies knowledge of the rules which we have shown him to be following and disavows all the intentions which we have recognized in his production; I do not consider this improbable. Then, however, only two possibilities remain. Either we have presented a veritable caricature of an interpretation, by putting into a harmless work of art tendencies of which its creator had no idea, and have thereby shown once again how easy it is to find what one seeks and what one is engrossed with—a possibility of which the strangest examples are recorded in the history of literature. Each reader may now decide for himself whether he cares to accept such an explanation; we, of course, stick to the other remaining view. We think that our author needed to know nothing of such rules and intentions, so that he may disavow them in good faith, and that we have found nothing in his romance that is not contained in it. We are probably drawing from the same source, working over the same material, each of us with a different method, and agreement in results seems to vouch for the fact that both have worked correctly. Our procedure consists in the conscious observation of abnormal psychic processes in others, in order to be able to discover and express their laws. Our author proceeds in another way; he directs his attention to the unconscious in his own psyche, is alive to its possibilities of development and grants them artistic expression, instead of suppressing them with conscious criticism. Thus he learns from himself what we learn from others—what laws the activity of this unconscious must follow. But he does not need to express these laws, need not even recognize them clearly; they are, as a result of the tolerance of his intellect, contained incarnate in his productions. We deduce these laws through an analysis of his fiction, just as we discover them from cases of real illness. But the conclusion seems irrefutable either that both—our author as well as the physician—have misunderstood the unconscious in the same way or that both have understood it correctly. This conclusion is very valuable for us; for its sake, it has been worth our while to investigate the representation of the formation and cure of the delusion as well as the dreams in Jensen's *Gradiva* by the methods of medical psychoanalysis.

We have reached the end. An observant reader might remind us that, at the beginning, we remarked that dreams are wishes represented as fulfilled and that we still owe the proof of it. Well, we reply, our arguments might well show how unjustifiable it would be to want to cover the explana-

tions which we have to give of dreams with the one formula
that the dream is a wish-fulfilment; but the assertion stands,
and is also easy to demonstrate for the dreams in *Gradiva*.
The latent dream-thoughts—we know now what is meant
by that—may be of the most diverse kinds. In *Gradiva* they
are "day's residues," thoughts which are left over unheard
and not disposed of by the psychic activity of waking life.
In order for a dream to originate from them, however, the
cooperation of a (generally unconscious) wish is required;
this supplies the driving power for the dream-formations;
the day's residues furnish the material for it.

In Norbert Hanold's first dream two wishes compete with
each other to produce the dream—one itself capable of
consciousness, the other, to be sure, belonging to the unconscious and active from repression. The first would be
the wish, natural for any archaeologist, to have been an eyewitness to that catastrophe of 79. What sacrifice would be
too great for an antiquarian to realize this wish otherwise
than through dreams! The other wish and dream-maker is
of an erotic nature: to be present when the beloved lies
down to sleep—to express it in crude or incomplete form.
It is the rejection of this which makes the dream an anxiety-
dream. Less striking, perhaps, are the impelling wishes of
the second dream; but if we recall its interpretation we shall
not hesitate to pronounce them erotic as well. The wish to
be captured by the beloved, to yield and surrender to her,
as it may be construed behind the lizard-catching, has really
a passive, masochistic character. On the next day the dreamer
strikes the beloved, as if under the sway of the antithetical
erotic force—but we must stop here, or we may actually
forget that Hanold and Gradiva are only creatures of our
author.

# APPENDIX TO THE SECOND EDITION

# OF "DELUSION AND DREAM"

In the five years that have passed since the writing of this study, psychoanalytic research has ventured to approach works of literature with another intention as well. It no longer seeks in these works merely a confirmation of its discoveries in unpoetic, neurotic individuals, but also demands to know out of what store of impressions and memories a creative writer has fashioned his work and in what way, through what processes, this material was introduced into the work of literature.

It has turned out that such questions can be answered most readily in the case of those writers who are wont to surrender, in naive joy of creating, to the urgings of their imagination, such as Wilhem Jensen, who died in 1911. Soon after the appearance of my analytic appraisal of his *Gradiva* I made an attempt to interest this elderly man of letters in these new tasks of psychoanalytic research; however, he declined to cooperate.

Since then a friend [1] has directed my attention to two other novellas by this author which probably have a genetic relationship to *Gradiva* as preliminary studies or earlier attempts to solve the same problem of the erotic life in a poetically satisfying manner. The first of these stories, entitled *Der rote Schirm* ("The Red Umbrella"), is reminiscent

[1] [Jung.—ED.]

of *Gradiva* in the recurrence of numerous little motifs—
the white death-flower, the forgotten object (Gradiva's
sketchbook), the meaningful little animal (the butterfly
and the lizard in *Gradiva*)—but especially in the repetition
of the basic situation, the appearance, in the midday heat
of summer, of a girl who is dead or believed to be dead.
The background for this apparition in *Der rote Schirm* is
supplied by the ruins of a castle, which is comparable to the
debris of excavated Pompeii in *Gradiva*.

The other novella, *Im gotischen Haus* ("In the Gothic
House"), has in its manifest content no such correspondence
with either *Gradiva* or *Der rote Schirm*. However, it was
given an external unity with the latter story by being published together with it in a volume entitled *Übermächte:
Zwei Novellen von Wilhelm Jensen* ("Superior Forces: Two
Novellas by Wilhelm Jensen"), Berlin, 1892. This fact is
an unmistakable indication of the latent kinship of these two
stories. It is easy to see that all three tales deal with the
same subject, namely, the development of a love affair (in
*Der rote Schirm* it is an inhibition of love) from the aftereffects of an intimate childhood association of the brother-
and-sister variety.

In a review which appeared in the Viennese daily *Die
Zeit* on February 11, 1912, Countess Eva Baudissin states
that Jensen's last novel, *Fremdlinge unter den Menschen*
("Strangers Among People"), which contains much material
from the author's own youth, relates the fate of a man
whose beloved turns out to be his sister.

In the two earlier novellas mentioned above there is no
trace of the basic motif of *Gradiva*—the strangely beautiful
walk with the perpendicularly lifted foot.

The relief which Jensen claims to be Roman and which is called "Gradiva" in the story is actually a product of the golden age of Greek art. It may be found as no. 644 in the Museo Chiaramonti in the Vatican; F. Hauser has restored it and published an interpretation of it ("Disiecta membra neuattischer Reliefs," in *Jahreshefte des österreichischen archäologischen Instituts*, Vol. VI, No. 1). Fitting the "Gradiva" relief together with other fragments in Florence and Munich yielded two relief plaques with three figures on each, in which may be recognized the Horae, the goddesses of vegetation, and the related deities of the fructifying dew.

# *The Relation of the Poet to Daydreaming*

We laymen have always wondered greatly—like the cardinal who put the question to Ariosto—how that strange being, the poet, comes by his material. What makes him able to carry us with him in such a way and to arouse emotions in us of which we thought ourselves perhaps not even capable? Our interest in the problem is only stimulated by the circumstance that if we ask poets themselves they give us no explanation of the matter, or at least no satisfactory explanation. The knowledge that not even the clearest insight into the factors conditioning the choice of imaginative material, or into the nature of the ability to fashion that material, will ever make writers of us does not in any way detract from our interest.

If we could only find some activity in ourselves, or in people like ourselves, which was in any way akin to the writing of imaginative works! If we could do so, then examination of it would give us a hope of obtaining some insight into the creative powers of imaginative writers. And indeed, there is some prospect of achieving this—writers themselves always try to lessen the distance between their kind and ordinary human beings; they so often assure us that every man is at heart a poet, and that the last poet will not die until the last human being does.

We ought surely to look in the child for the first traces of imaginative activity. The child's best-loved and most absorbing occupation is play. Perhaps we may say that every child at play behaves like an imaginative writer, in that he creates a world of his own or, more truly, he rearranges the things of his world and orders it in a new way that pleases him better. It would be incorrect to think that he does not take this world seriously; on the contrary, he takes his play very seriously and expends a great deal of emotion on it. The opposite of play is not serious occupation but—reality. Notwithstanding the large affective cathexis of his play-world, the child distinguishes it perfectly from reality; only he likes to borrow the objects and circumstances that he imagines from the tangible and visible things of the real world. It is only this linking of it to reality that still distinguishes a child's "play" from "daydreaming."

Now the writer does the same as the child at play; he creates a world of fantasy which he takes very seriously; that is, he invests it with a great deal of affect, while separating it sharply from reality. Language has preserved this relationship between children's play and poetic creation. It designates certain kinds of imaginative creation, concerned with tangible objects and capable of representation, as "plays"; the people who present them are called "players." The unreality of this poetical world of imagination, however, has very important consequences for literary technique; for many things which if they happened in real life could produce no pleasure can nevertheless give enjoyment in a play—many emotions which are essentially painful may become a source of enjoyment to the spectators and hearers of a poet's work.

There is another consideration relating to the contrast between reality and play on which we will dwell for a moment. Long after a child has grown up and stopped playing, after he has for decades attempted to grasp the realities of life with all seriousness, he may one day come to a state of mind in which the contrast between play and reality is again abrogated. The adult can remember with what intense seriousness he carried on his childish play; then by comparing his would-be serious occupations with his childhood's play, he manages to throw off the heavy burden of life and obtain the great pleasure of humor.

As they grow up, people cease to play, and appear to give up the pleasure they derived from play. But anyone who knows anything of the mental life of human beings is aware that hardly anything is more difficult to them than to give up a pleasure they have once tasted. Really we never can relinquish anything; we only exchange one thing for something else. When we appear to give something up, all we really do is to adopt a substitute. So when the human being grows up and ceases to play he only gives up the connection with real objects; instead of playing he then begins to create fantasy. He builds castles in the air and creates what are called daydreams. I believe that the greater number of human beings create fantasies at times as long as they live. This is a fact which has been overlooked for a long time, and its importance has therefore not been properly appreciated.

The fantasies of human beings are less easy to observe than the play of children. Children do, it is true, play alone, or form with other children a closed world in their minds for the purposes of play; but a child does not conceal his play from adults, even though his playing is quite unconcerned with them. The adult, on the other hand, is ashamed of his daydreams and conceals them from other people; he cherishes them as his most intimate possessions, and as a rule he would rather confess all his misdeeds than tell his daydreams. For this reason he may believe that he is the only person who makes up such fantasies, without having any idea that everybody else tells himself stories of the same kind. Daydreaming is a continuation of play, nevertheless, and the motives which lie behind these two activities contain a very good reason for this different behavior in the child at play and in the daydreaming adult.

The play of children is determined by their wishes—really by the child's *one* wish, which is to be grown-up, the wish that helps to "bring him up." He always plays at being grown-up; in play he imitates what is known to him of the lives of adults. Now he has no reason to conceal this wish. With the adult it is otherwise; on the one hand, he knows that he is expected not to play any longer or to daydream, but to be making his way in a real world. On the other hand, some of the wishes from which his fantasies spring are such as have to be entirely hidden; therefore he is ashamed of his fantasies as being childish and as something prohibited.

If they are concealed with so much secretiveness, you will ask, how do we know so much about the human propensity to create fantasies? Now there is a certain class of human beings upon whom not a god, indeed, but a stern goddess—Necessity—has laid the task of giving an account of what they suffer and what they enjoy. These people are the neurotics; among other things they have to confess their fantasies to the physician to whom they go in the hope of recovering through mental treatment. This is our best source of knowledge, and we have later found good reason to suppose that our patients tell us about themselves nothing that we could not also hear from healthy people.

Let us try to learn some of the characteristics of day-dreaming. We can begin by saying that happy people never make fantasies, only unsatisfied ones. Unsatisfied wishes are the driving power behind fantasies; every separate fantasy contains the fulfillment of a wish, and improves on unsatisfactory reality. The impelling wishes vary according to the sex, character, and circumstances of the creator; they may be easily divided, however, into two principal groups. Either they are ambitious wishes, serving to exalt the person creating them, or they are erotic. In young women erotic wishes dominate the fantasies almost exclusively, for their ambition is generally comprised in their erotic longings; in young men egoistic and ambitious wishes assert themselves plainly enough alongside their erotic desires. But we will not lay stress on the distinction between these two trends; we prefer to emphasize the fact that they are often united. In many altarpieces the portrait of the donor is to be found in one corner of the picture; and in the greater number of ambitious daydreams, too, we can discover a woman in some corner, for whom the dreamer performs all his heroic deeds and at whose feet all his triumphs are to be laid. Here you see we have strong enough motives for concealment; a well-brought-up woman is, indeed, credited with only a minimum of erotic desire, while a young man has to learn to suppress the overweening self-regard he acquires in the indulgent atmosphere surrounding his childhood, so that he may find his proper place in a society that is full of other persons making similar claims.

We must not imagine that the various products of this impulse towards fantasy, castles in the air or daydreams, are stereotyped or unchangeable. On the contrary, they fit themselves into the changing impressions of life, alter with the vicissitudes of life; every deep new impression gives them what might be called a "date-stamp." The relation of fantasies to time is altogether of great importance. One may say that a fantasy at one and the same moment hovers between three periods of time—the three periods of our ideation. The activity of fantasy in the mind is linked up with some current impression, occasioned by some event in the present, which had the power to rouse an intense desire. From there it wanders back to the memory of an early experience, generally belonging to infancy, in which this wish was fulfilled. Then it creates for itself a situation which is to emerge in the future, representing the fulfillment of the wish—this is the daydream or fantasy, which now carries in it traces both of the occasion which engendered it and of some past memory. So past, present, and future are threaded, as it were, on the string of the wish that runs through them all.

A very ordinary example may serve to make my statement clearer. Take the case of a poor orphan lad, to whom you have given the address of some employer where he may perhaps get work. On the way there he falls into a daydream suitable to the situation from which it springs. The content of the fantasy will be somewhat as follows: He is taken on and pleases his new employer, makes himself indispensable in the business, is taken into the family of the employer, and marries the charming daughter of the house. Then he comes to conduct the business, first as a partner, and then as successor to his father-in-law. In this way the dreamer regains what he had in his happy childhood, the protecting house, his loving parents, and the first objects of his affection. You will see from such an example how the wish employs some event in the present to plan a future on the pattern of the past.

Much more could be said about fantasies, but I will only allude as briefly as possible to certain points. If fantasies become over-luxuriant and over-powerful, the necessary conditions for an outbreak of neurosis or psychosis are constituted; fantasies are also the first preliminary stage in the mind of the symptoms of illness of which our patients complain. A broad bypath here branches off into pathology.

I cannot pass over the relation of fantasies to dreams. Our nocturnal dreams are nothing but such fantasies, as we can make clear by interpreting them.[1] Language, in its unrivaled wisdom, long ago decided the question of the essential nature of dreams by giving the name of "daydreams" to the airy creations of fantasy. If the meaning of our dreams usually remains obscure in spite of this clue, it is because of the circumstance that at night wishes of which we are ashamed also become active in us, wishes which we have to hide from ourselves, which were consequently repressed and pushed back into the unconscious. Such repressed wishes and their derivatives can therefore achieve expression only when almost completely disguised. When

[1] Cf. Freud, *The Interpretation of Dreams.*

scientific work had succeeded in elucidating the distortion in dreams, it was no longer difficult to recognize that nocturnal dreams are fulfillments of desires in exactly the same way as daydreams are—those fantasies with which we are all so familiar.

So much for daydreaming; now for the poet! Shall we dare really to compare an imaginative writer with "one who dreams in broad daylight," and his creations with daydreams? Here, surely, a first distinction is forced upon us; we must distinguish between poets who, like the bygone creators of epics and tragedies, take over their material ready-made, and those who seem to create their material spontaneously. Let us keep to the latter, and let us also not choose for our comparison those writers who are most highly esteemed by critics. We will choose the less pretentious writers of romances, novels, and stories, who are read all the same by the widest circles of men and women. There is one very marked characteristic in the productions of these writers which must strike us all: they all have a hero who is the center of interest, for whom the author tries to win our sympathy by every possible means, and whom he places under the protection of a special providence. If at the end of one chapter the hero is left unconscious and bleeding from severe wounds, I am sure to find him at the beginning of the next being carefully tended and on the way to recovery; if the first volume ends in the hero being shipwrecked in a storm at sea, I am certain to hear at the beginning of the next of his hairbreadth escape—otherwise, indeed, the story could not continue. The feeling of security with which I follow the hero through his dangerous adventures is the same as that with which a real hero throws himself into the water to save a drowning man, or exposes himself to the fire of the enemy while storming a battery. It is this very feeling of being a hero which one of our best authors has well expressed in the famous phrase, *"Es kann dir nix g'schehen!"* [2] It seems to me, however, that this significant mark of invulnerability very clearly betrays—His Majesty the Ego, the hero of all daydreams and all novels.

The same relationship is hinted at in yet other characteristics of these egocentric stories. When all the women in a novel invariably fall in love with the hero, this can hardly be looked upon as a description of reality; but it is easily understood as an essential constituent of a daydream. The same thing holds good when the other people in the story are sharply divided into good and bad, with complete disregard of the manifold variety in the traits of real human beings; the "good" ones are those who help the ego in its character of hero, while the "bad" are his enemies and rivals.

We do not in any way fail to recognize that many imaginative productions have traveled far from the original naive daydream, but I cannot suppress the surmise that even the most extreme variations could be brought into relationship with this model by an uninterrupted series of transitions. It has struck me in many so-called psychological novels, too, that only one person—once again the hero—is described from within; the author dwells in his soul and looks upon the other people from outside. The psychological novel in general probably owes its peculiarities to the tendency of modern writers to split up their ego by self-observation into many component egos, and in this way to personify the conflicting trends in their own mental life in many heroes. There

---

[2] Anzengruber. [The phrase means: "Nothing can happen to *me!*"— TRANS.]

are certain novels, which might be called "excentric," that seem to stand in marked contradiction to the typical daydream; in these the person introduced as the hero plays the least active part of anyone, and seems instead to let the actions and sufferings of other people pass him by like a spectator. Many of the later novels of Zola belong to this class. But I must say that the psychological analysis of people who are not writers, and who deviate in many things from the so-called norm, has shown us analogous variations in their daydreams in which the ego contents itself with the role of spectator.

If our comparison of the imaginative writer with the daydreamer, and of poetic production with the daydream, is to be of any value, it must show itself fruitful in some way or other. Let us try, for instance, to examine the works of writers in reference to the idea propounded above, the relation of the fantasy to the wish that runs through it and to the three periods of time; and with its help let us study the connection between the life of the writer and his productions. Hitherto it has not been known what preliminary ideas would constitute an approach to this problem; very often this relation has been regarded as much simpler than it is; but the insight gained from fantasies leads us to expect the following state of things. Some actual experience which made a strong impression on the writer had stirred up a memory of an earlier experience, generally belonging to childhood, which then arouses a wish that finds a fulfillment in the work in question, and in which elements of the recent event and the old memory should be discernible.

Do not be alarmed at the complexity of this formula; I myself expect that in reality it will prove itself to be too schematic, but that possibly it may contain a first means of approach to the true state of affairs. From some attempts I have made I think that this way of approaching works of the imagination might not be unfruitful. You will not forget that the stress laid on the writer's memories of his childhood, which perhaps seems so strange, is ultimately derived from the hypothesis that imaginative creation, like daydreaming, is a continuation of and substitute for the play of childhood.

We will not neglect to refer also to that class of imaginative work which must be recognized not as spontaneous production, but as a refashioning of ready-made material. Here, too, the writer retains a certain amount of independence, which can express itself in the choice of material and in changes in the material chosen, which are often considerable. As far as it goes, this material is derived from the racial treasure-house of myths, legends, and fairy tales. The study of these creations of racial psychology is in no way complete, but it seems extremely probable that myths, for example, are distorted vestiges of the wish-fantasies of whole nations—the agelong dreams of young humanity.

You will say that, although writers came first in the title of this paper, I have told you far less about them than about fantasy. I am aware of that, and will try to excuse myself by pointing to the present state of our knowledge. I could only throw out suggestions and bring up interesting points which arise from the study of fantasies, and which pass beyond them to the problem of the choice of literary material. We have not touched on the other problem at all— i.e., what are the means which writers use to achieve those emotional reactions in us that are roused by their productions. But I would at least point out to you the path which leads from our discussion of daydreams to the problems of the effect produced on us by imaginative works.

You will remember that we said the daydreamer hid his fantasies carefully from other people because he had reason to be ashamed of them. I may now add that even if he were to communicate them to us, he would give us no pleasure by his disclosures. When we hear such fantasies they repel us, or at least leave us cold. But when a man of literary talent presents his plays, or relates what we take to be his personal daydreams, we experience great pleasure arising probably from many sources. How the writer accomplishes this is his innermost secret; the essential *ars poetica* lies in the technique by which our feeling of repulsion is overcome, and this has certainly to do with those barriers erected between every individual being and all others. We can guess at two methods used in this technique. The writer softens the egotistical character of the daydream by changes and disguises, and he bribes us by the offer of a purely formal—that is, aesthetic—pleasure in the presentation of his fantasies. The increment of pleasure which is offered us in order to release yet greater pleasure arising from deeper sources in the mind is called an "incitement premium" or, technically, "fore-pleasure." I am of opinion that all the aesthetic pleasure we gain from the works of imaginative writers is of the same type as this "fore-pleasure," and that the true enjoyment of literature proceeds from the release of tensions in our minds. Perhaps much that brings about this result consists in the writer's putting us into a position in which we can enjoy our own daydreams without reproach or shame. Here we reach a path leading into novel, interesting, and complicated researches, but we also, at least for the present, arrive at the end of the present discussion.

# The Occurrence in Dreams
## of Material from Fairy Tales

It it not surprising to find that psychoanalysis confirms us in our recognition of how great an influence folk fairy tales have upon the mental life of our children. In some people a recollection of their favorite fairy tales takes the place of memories of their own childhood: they have made the fairy tales into screen-memories.

Elements and situations derived from fairy tales are also frequently to be found in dreams. In interpreting those portions of the dreams the patient will produce the significant fairy tale as an association. In the present paper I shall give two instances of this very common occurrence. But it will not be possible to do more than hint at the relation of the fairy tales to the history of the dreamer's childhood and to his neurosis, though this limitation will involve the risk of snapping threads which were of the utmost importance in the analysis.

I

Here is a dream of a young married woman (who had had a visit from her husband a few days before): *She was in a room that was entirely brown. A little door led to the top of a steep staircase, and up this staircase there came into the room a curious manikin—small, with white hair, a bald top to his head, and a red nose.* He danced round the room in front of her, carried on in the funniest way, and then went down the staircase again. He was dressed in a grey garment, through which his whole figure was visible. (A correction was made subsequently: *He was wearing a long black coat and grey trousers.*)

The analysis was as follows. The description of the manikin's personal appearance fitted the dreamer's father-in-law without any alteration being necessary.[1] Immediately afterwards, however, the story of "Rumpelstiltskin" occurred to her; for he danced around in the same funny way as the man in the dream and in so doing betrayed his name to the queen. But by that he also lost his claim upon the queen's first child, and in his fury he tore himself in two.

On the day before she had the dream she herself had been furious with her husband and had exclaimed: "I could tear him in two."

The brown room at first gave rise to difficulties. All that occurred to her was her parents' dining room, which was paneled in that color—in brown wood. She then told some stories of beds which were so uncomfortable for two people to sleep in. A few days before, when the subject of conversation had been beds in other countries, she had said something very *mal à propos*—quite innocently, as she maintained—and everyone in the room had roared with laughter.

The dream was now already intelligible. The brown wood room[2] was in the first place a bed, and through the connec-

---

[1] Except for the detail that the manikin had his hair cut short, whereas her father-in-law wore his long.

[2] Wood, as is well known, is frequently a female or maternal symbol: e.g., *materia, Madeira*, etc.

tion with the dining room it was a double bed.[3] She was therefore in her double bed. Her visitor should have been her young husband, who, after an absence of several months, had visited her to play his part in the double bed. But to begin with it was her husband's father, her father-in-law.

Behind this interpretation we have a glimpse of a deeper and purely sexual content. The room, at this level, was the vagina. (The room was in her—this was reversed in the dream.) The little man who made grimaces and behaved so funnily was the penis. The narrow door and the steep stairs confirmed the view that the situation was a representation of coitus. As a rule we are accusomed to find the penis symbolized by a child; but we shall find that there was good reason for a father being introduced to represent the penis in this instance.

The solution of the remaining portion of the dream will entirely confirm us in this interpretation. The dreamer herself explained the transparent grey garment as a condom. We may gather that considerations of preventing conception and worries whether this visit of her husband's might not have sown the seed of a second child were among the instigating causes of the dream.

*The black coat.* Coats of that kind suited her husband admirably. She was eager to influence him always to wear them, instead of his usual clothes. Dressed in the black coat, therefore, her husband was as she would like to see him. *The black coat and the grey trousers.* At two different levels, one above the other, this had the same meaning: "I should like you to be dressed like that. I like you like that."

---

[3] Literally, "marriage-bed." For table and bed stand for marriage. [Cf. the legal phrase: *a mensa et toro.*—ED.]

Rumpelstiltskin was connected with the contemporary thoughts underlying the dream—the day's residue—by a neat antithetic relation. He comes in the fairy tale in order to take away the queen's first child. The little man in the dream comes in the shape of a father, because he has presumably brought a second child. But Rumpelstiltskin also gave access to the deeper, infantile stratum of the dream-thoughts. The droll little fellow, whose very name is unknown; whose secret is so eagerly canvassed; who can perform such extraordinary tricks (in the fairy tale he turns straw into gold), the fury against him, or rather against his possessor, who is envied for possessing him (the penis-envy felt by girls)—all of these are elements whose relation to the foundations of the patient's neurosis can, as I have said, barely be touched upon in this paper. The short-cut hair of the manikin in the dream was no doubt also connected with the subject of castration.

If we carefully observe from clear instances the way in which the dreamer uses the fairy tale and the point at which he brings it in, we may perhaps also succeed in picking up some hints which will help in interpreting any remaining obscurities in the fairy tale itself.

II

A young man[4] told me the following dream. He had a chronological basis for his early memories in the circumstance that his parents moved from one country estate to another just before the end of his fifth year; the dream, which he said was his earliest one, occurred while he was still upon the first estate.

[4] [A detailed analysis of this patient's case will be found in "From the History of an Infantile Neurosis," *Collected Papers*, Vol. III.—Trans.]

*"I dreamt that it was night and that I was lying in my bed. (My bed stood with its foot towards the window; in front of the window there was a row of old walnut trees. I know it was winter when I had the dream, and night time.) Suddenly the window opened of its own accord, and I was terrified to see that some white wolves were sitting on the big walnut tree in front of the window. There were six or seven of them. The wolves were quite white; and looked more like foxes or sheep dogs, for they had big tails like foxes and they had their ears pricked like dogs when they are attending to something. In great terror, evidently of being eaten up by the wolves, I screamed* and woke up. My nurse hurried to my bed, to see what had happened to me. It took quite a long while before I was convinced that it had only been a dream; I had had such a clear and life-like picture of the window opening and the wolves sitting on the tree. At last I grew quieter, felt as though I had escaped from some danger, and went to sleep again.*

"The only piece of action in the dream was the opening of the window; for the wolves sat quite still and without any movement on the branches of the tree, to the right and left of the trunk, and looked at me. It seemed as though they had riveted their whole attention upon me.—I think this was my first anxiety-dream. I was three, four, or at most five years old at the time. From then until my eleventh or twelfth year I was always afraid of seeing something terrible in my dreams."

He added a drawing of the tree with the wolves, which confirmed his description. The analysis of the dream brought the following material to light.

He had always connected this dream with the recollection

that during these years of his childhood he was most tre-
mendously afraid of the picture of a wolf in a book of fairy
tales. His elder sister, who was very much his superior, used
to tease him by holding up this particular picture in front
of him on some excuse or other, so that he was terrified and
began to scream. In this picture the wolf was standing upright, striding out with one foot, with its claws stretched out
and its ears pricked. He thought this picture must have been
an illustration to the story of "Little Red Riding Hood."

Why were the wolves white? This made him think of the
sheep, large flocks of which were kept in the neighborhood
of the estate. His father occasionally took him to visit these
flocks, and every time this happened he felt very proud
and blissful. Later on—according to inquiries that were
made, it may easily have been shortly before the time of the
dream—an epidemic broke out among the sheep. His father
sent for a follower of Pasteur, who inoculated the animals,
but after the inoculation even more of them died than before.

How did the wolves come to be on the tree? This reminded
him of a story that he had heard his grandfather tell. He
could not remember whether it was before or after the
dream, but its subject is a decisive argument in favor of the
former view. The story ran as follows. A tailor was sitting
at work in his room, when the window opened and a wolf
leapt in. The tailor hit at him with his yard—no (he cor-
rected himself), caught him by his tail and pulled it off, so
that the wolf ran away in terror. Some time later the tailor
went into the forest, and suddenly saw a pack of wolves
coming towards him; so he climbed up a tree to escape from
them. At first the wolves were in perplexity; but the maimed

one, which was among them and wanted to revenge himself upon the tailor, proposed that they should climb one upon another till the last one could reach him. He himself—he was a vigorous old fellow—would be the base of the pyramid. The wolves did as he suggested, but the tailor had recognized the visitor whom he had punished, and suddenly called out as he had before: "Catch the grey one by his tail!" The tailless wolf, terrified by the recollection, ran away, and all the others tumbled down.

In this story the tree appears, upon which the wolves were sitting in the dream. But it also contains an unmistakable allusion to the castration complex. The *old* wolf was docked of his tail by the tailor. The foxtails of the wolves in the dream were probably compensations for this taillessness.

Why were there six or seven wolves? There seemed to be no answer to this question, until I raised a doubt whether the picture that had frightened him could be connected with the story of "Little Red Riding Hood." This fairy tale offers an opportunity for only two illustrations—Little Red Riding Hood's meeting with the wolf in the wood, and the scene in which the wolf lies in bed in the grandmother's nightcap. There must therefore be some other fairy tale behind his recollection of the picture. He soon discovered that it could only be the story of "The Wolf and the Seven Little Goats." Here the number seven occurs, and also the number six, for the wolf ate up only six of the little goats, while the seventh hid itself in the clock-case. The white, too, comes into this story, for the wolf had his paw made white at the baker's after the little goats had recognized him on his first visit by his grey paw. Moreover, the two fairy tales have much in common. In both there is the eating up, the cutting open of the belly, the taking out of the people who have been eaten and their replacement by heavy stones, and finally in both of them the wicked wolf perishes. Besides all this, in the story of the little goats the tree appears. The wolf lay down under a tree after his meal and snored.

I shall have, for a special reason, to deal with this dream again elsewhere, and interpret it and consider its significance in greater detail. For it is the earliest anxiety-dream that the dreamer remembered from his childhood, and its content, taken in connection with other dreams that followed it soon afterwards and with certain events in his earliest years, is of quite peculiar interest. We must confine ourselves here to the relation of the dream to the two fairy tales which have so much in common with each other, "Little Red Riding Hood" and "The Wolf and the Seven Little Goats." The effect produced by these stories was shown in the little dreamer by a regular animal-phobia. This phobia was only distinguished from other similar cases by the fact that the anxiety-animal was not an object easily accessible to observation (such as a horse or a dog), but was known to him only from stories and picture-books.

I shall discuss on another occasion the explanation of these animal-phobias and the significance attaching to them. I will only remark in anticipation that this explanation is in complete harmony with the principal characteristic shown by the neurosis from which the present dreamer suffered in the later part of his life. His fear of his father was the strongest motive for his falling ill, and his ambivalent attitude towards every father-surrogate was the dominating feature of his life as well as of his behavior during the treatment.

If in my patient's case the wolf was merely a first father-surrogate, the question arises whether the hidden content in the fairy tales of the wolf that ate up the little goats and of "Little Red Riding Hood" may not simply be infantile fear of the father.[5] Moreover, my patient's father had the characteristic, shown by so many people in relation to their children, of indulging in "affectionate abuse"; and it is possible that during the patient's earlier years his father (though he grew severe later on) may more than once, as he caressed the little boy or played with him, have threatened in fun to "gobble him up." One of my patients told me that her two children could never get to be fond of their grandfather, because in the course of his affectionate romping with them he used to frighten them by saying he would cut open their tummies.

[5] Compare the similarity between these two fairy tales and the myth of Cronos, which was pointed out by Rank in his paper, "Völkerpsychologische Parallelen zu den infantilen Sexualtheorien" (1912).

# A Connection Between a Symbol and a Symptom

The hat has been adequately established as a symbol of the genital organ, most frequently the male, through analyses of dreams. It cannot be said, however, that this symbol is at all an intelligible one. In fantasies and in numerous symptoms the head also appears as a symbol of the male genitals, or, if one prefers to put it so, as a representation of them. Many analysts will have noticed that certain patients suffering from obsessions express an abhorrence of and indignation against the penalty of beheading, feelings which are far more pronounced as regards this than any other form of capital punishment, and will in consequence have had to explain to them that they treat being beheaded as a substitute for being castrated. Dreams of young people or dreams occurring during the period of youth which concern the subject of castration, and in which there was mention of a ball which could only be interpreted as the head of the dreamer's father, have been often analyzed and frequently published. I have recently been able to solve a ceremonial carried out by a patient before going to sleep, which consisted in laying a small pillow diamond-wise on a larger one so that the sleeper's head would rest exactly in the long diameter of the diamond. The diamond had the meaning that is familiar

143

to us from drawings on walls; the head was to represent the male organ.

It may be that the symbolic meaning of the hat is derived from that of the head, in so far as the hat can be considered as a continuation of the head, though detachable. In this connection I call to mind a symptom of obsessional neurotics by means of which they manage to ensure themselves continual torment. When they are in the street they are constantly watching to see whether some acquaintance will salute them first, by taking off his hat, or whether he seems to wait for their salute; and they give up a number of their acquaintances who they imagine no longer salute them or do not return their salute properly. There is no end to their perplexities on the point; they find them everywhere as their mood and fancy dictate. It makes no difference to their behavior when we tell them, what they all know already, that the salute by taking off the hat signifies an abasement before the saluted person, that a Spanish grandee, for example, enjoyed the privilege of being in the presence of the king with his head covered; and that their sensitiveness to saluting has therefore the meaning of not being willing to show themselves as of less importance than the other person thinks himself to be. The resistance of their sensitiveness to such an explanation suggests the activity of a motive less present to consciousness, and the source of this excess of feeling can easily be found in relation to the castration complex.

# GRADIVA: A POMPEIIAN FANCY

by
Wilhelm Jensen

APPENDIX

GRADIVA: A POMPEIAN FANCY

by

Wilhelm Jensen

# Gradiva: A Pompeiian Fancy

On a visit to one of the great antique collections of Rome, Norbert Hanold had discovered a bas-relief which was exceptionally attractive to him; so he was much pleased, after his return to Germany, to be able to get a splendid plaster cast of it. This had now been hanging for some years on one of the walls of his workroom, all the other walls of which were lined with bookcases. Here it had the advantage of a position with the right light exposure, on a wall visited, though but briefly, by the evening sun.

About one-third life-size, the bas-relief represented a complete female figure in the act of walking; she was still young, but no longer in childhood and, on the other hand, apparently not a woman, but a Roman virgin about in her twentieth year. In no way did she remind one of the numerous extant bas-reliefs of a Venus, a Diana, or other Olympian goddess, and equally little of a Psyche or nymph. In her was embodied something humanly commonplace—not in a bad sense—to a degree a sense of present time, as if the artist, instead of making a pencil sketch of her on a sheet of paper, as is done in our day, had fixed her in a clay model quickly, from life, as she passed on the street, a tall, slight figure, whose soft, wavy hair a folded kerchief almost completely bound. Her rather slender face was not at all dazzling, and the desire to produce such effect was obviously equally foreign to her; in the delicately formed features was expressed a nonchalant equanimity in regard to what was occurring about her; her eye, which gazed calmly ahead, bespoke absolutely unimpaired powers of vision and thoughts quietly withdrawn.

So the young woman was fascinating, not at all because of plastic beauty of form, but because she possessed something rare in antique sculpture—a realistic, simple, maidenly grace which gave the impression of imparting life to the relief. This was effected chiefly by the movement represented in the picture. With her head bent forward a little, she held slightly raised in her left hand, so that her sandaled feet became visible, her garment, which fell in exceedingly voluminous folds from her throat to her ankles. The left foot had advanced, and the right, about to follow, touched the ground only lightly with the tips of the toes, while the sole and heel were raised almost vertically. This movement produced a double impression of exceptional agility and of confident composure, and the flight-like poise, combined with a firm step, lent her the peculiar grace.

Where had she walked thus and whither was she going? Dr. Norbert Hanold, docent of archaeology, really found in the relief nothing noteworthy for his science. It was not a plastic production of great art of the ancient times, but essentially a Roman genre production; and he could not explain what quality in it had aroused his attention. He knew only that he had been attracted by something, and this effect of the first view had remained unchanged since then. In order to bestow a name upon the piece of sculpture, he had called it to himself Gradiva, "the girl splendid in walking." That was an epithet applied by the ancient poets solely to Mars Gradivus, the war-god going out to battle. Yet to Norbert it seemed the most appropriate designation for the bearing and movement of the young girl, or, according to the expression of our day, of the young lady; for obviously she did not belong to a lower class but was the daughter of a nobleman, or at any rate was of honorable family. Perhaps—her appearance brought the idea to his mind involuntarily—she might be of the family of a patrician aedile, whose office was connected with the worship of Ceres, and she was on her way to the temple of the goddess on some errand.

Yet it was contrary to the young archaeologist's feeling to put her in the frame of great, noisy, cosmopolitan Rome. To his mind, her calm, quiet manner did not belong in this complex machine, where no one heeded another. She belonged rather in a smaller place, where everyone knew her and, stopping to glance after her, said to a companion, "That is Gradiva"—her real name Norbert could not supply—"the daughter of ———. She walks more beautifully than any other girl in our city."

As if he had heard it thus with his own ears, the idea had become firmly rooted in his mind, where another supposition had developed almost into a conviction. On his Italian journey he had spent several weeks in Pompeii studying the ruins. And in Germany the idea had suddenly come to him one day that the girl depicted by the relief was walking there, somewhere, on the peculiar steppingstones which have been excavated; these had made a dry crossing possible in rainy weather, but had afforded passage for chariot-wheels. Thus he saw her putting one foot across the interstice while the other was about to follow, and, as he contemplated the

girl, her immediate and more remote environment rose
before his imagination like an actuality. It created for him,
with the aid of his knowledge of antiquity, the vista of a
long street, among the houses of which were many temples
and porticoes. Different kinds of business and trades, stalls,
workshops, taverns came into view; bakers had their breads
on display; earthenware jugs, set into marble counters,
offered everything requisite for household and kitchen. At
the street corner sat a woman offering vegetables and fruit
for sale from baskets; from a half-dozen large walnuts she
had removed half of the shells to show the meat, fresh and
sound, as a temptation for purchasers. Wherever the eye
turned, it fell upon lively colors, gaily painted wall surfaces,
pillars with red and yellow capitals; everything reflected the
glitter and glare of the dazzling noonday sun. Farther off
on a high base rose a gleaming white statue, above which,
in the distance, half veiled by the tremulous vibrations of
the hot air, loomed Mount Vesuvius, not yet in its present
cone shape and brown aridity, but covered to its furrowed,
rocky peak with glistening verdure. In the street only a few
people moved about, seeking shade wherever possible, for
the scorching heat of the summer noon hour paralyzed the
usually bustling activities. There Gradiva walked over the
steppingstones and scared away from them a shimmering
golden-green lizard.

Thus the picture stood vividly before Norbert Hanold's
eyes; but, from daily contemplation of her head, another
new conjecture had gradually arisen. The cut of her features
seemed to him, more and more, not Roman or Latin, but
Greek, so that her Hellenic ancestry gradually became for
him a certainty. The ancient settlement of all southern Italy

by Greeks offered sufficient ground for that, and more ideas pleasantly associated with the settlers developed. Then the young "domina" had perhaps spoken Greek in her parental home, and had grown up fostered by Greek culture. Upon closer consideration he found this also confirmed by the expression of the face, for quite decidedly wisdom and a delicate spirituality lay hidden beneath her modesty.

These conjectures or discoveries could, however, establish no real archaeological interest in the little relief, and Norbert was well aware that something else, which no doubt might be under the head of science, made him return to frequent contemplation of the likeness. For him it was a question of critical judgment as to whether the artist had reproduced Gradiva's manner of walking from life. About that he could not become absolutely certain, and his rich collection of copies of antique plastic works did not help him in this matter. The nearly vertical position of the right foot seemed exaggerated; in all experiments which he himself made, the movement left his rising foot always in a much less upright position; mathematically formulated, his stood, during the brief moment of lingering, at an angle of only forty-five degrees from the ground, and this seemed to him natural for the mechanics of walking, because it served the purpose best. Once he used the presence of a young anatomist friend as an opportunity for raising the question; but the latter was not able to deliver a definite decision, as he had made no observations in this connection. He confirmed the experience of his friend as agreeing with his own, but could not say whether a woman's manner of walking was different from that of a man, and the question remained unanswered.

In spite of this, the discussion had not been without profit, for it suggested something that had not formerly occurred to him; namely, observation from life for the purpose of enlightenment on the matter. That forced him, to be sure, to a mode of action utterly foreign to him; women had formerly been for him only a conception in marble or bronze, and he had never given his female contemporaries the least consideration. But his desire for knowledge transported him into a scientific passion in which he surrendered himself to the peculiar investigation which he recognized as necessary. This was hindered by many difficulties in the human throng of the large city, and results of the research were to be hoped for only in the less frequented streets. Yet, even there, long skirts generally made the mode of walking undiscernible, for almost no one but housemaids wore short skirts and they, with the exception of a few, because of their heavy shoes could not well be considered in solving the question. In spite of this he steadfastly continued his survey in dry as well as wet weather; he perceived that the latter promised the quickest results, for it caused the ladies to raise their skirts. To many ladies, his searching glances directed at their feet must have inevitably been quite noticeable; sometimes a displeased expression of the lady observed showed that she considered his demeanor a mark of boldness or ill-breeding; sometimes, as he was a young man of very captivating appearance, the opposite, a bit of encouragement, was expressed by a pair of eyes. Yet one was as incomprehensible to him as the other.

Gradually his perseverance resulted in the collection of a considerable number of observations, which brought to his attention many differences. Some walked slowly, some fast, some ponderously, some buoyantly. Many let their soles

merely glide over the ground; not many raised them more
obliquely to a smarter position. Among all, however, not a
single one presented to view Gradiva's manner of walking.
This filled him with satisfaction that he had not been mis-
taken in his archaeological judgment of the relief. On the
other hand, his observations caused him annoyance, for he
found the vertical position of the lingering foot beautiful,
and regretted that it had been created by the imagination
or arbitrary act of the sculptor and did not correspond to
reality.

Soon after his pedestrian investigations had yielded him
this knowledge, he had, one night, a dream which caused
him great anguish of mind. In it he was in old Pompeii, and
on the twenty-fourth of August of the year 79 A.D., which
witnessed the eruption of Vesuvius. The heavens held the
doomed city wrapped in a black mantle of smoke; only here
and there the flaring masses of flame from the crater made
distinguishable, through a rift, something steeped in blood-
red light; all the inhabitants, either individually or in confused crowds, stunned out of their senses by the unusual
horror, sought safety in flight. The pebbles and the rain of
ashes fell down on Norbert also, but, after the strange manner of dreams, they did not hurt him; and, in the same way,
he smelled the deadly sulphur fumes of the air without
having his breathing impeded by them. As he stood thus
at the edge of the Forum near the Temple of Jupiter, he
suddenly saw Gradiva a short distance in front of him.
Until then no thought of her presence there had moved him,
but now suddenly it seemed natural to him, as she was, of
course, a Pompeiian girl, that she was living in her native
city and, without his having any suspicion of it, was his

contemporary. He recognized her at first glance; the stone model of her was splendidly striking in every detail, even to her gait; involuntarily he designated this as *lente festinans.* So with buoyant composure and the calm unmindfulness of her surroundings peculiar to her, she walked across the flag-stones of the Forum to the Temple of Apollo. She seemed not to notice the impending fate of the city, but to be given up to her thoughts; on that account he also forgot the fright-ful occurrence, for at least a few moments, and because of a feeling that the living reality would quickly disappear from him again, he tried to impress it accurately on his mind. Then, however, he became suddenly aware that if she did not quickly save herself, she must perish in the general de-struction, and violent fear forced from him a cry of warning. She heard it, too, for her head turned toward him so that her face now appeared for a moment in full view, yet with an utterly uncomprehending expression; and, without paying any more attention to him, she continued in the same direc-tion as before. At the same time, her face became paler as if it were changing to white marble; she stepped up to the portico of the Temple, and then, between the pillars, she sat down on a step and slowly laid her head upon it. Now the pebbles were falling in such masses that they condensed into a completely opaque curtain; hastening quickly after her, however, he found his way to the place where she had disappeared from his view, and there she lay, protected by the projecting roof, stretched out on the broad step, as if for sleep, but no longer breathing, apparently stifled by the sulphur fumes. From Vesuvius the red glow flared over her countenance, which, with closed eyes, was exactly like that of a beautiful statue. No fear nor distortion was apparent, but a strange equanimity, calmly submitting to the inevitable, was manifest in her features. Yet they quickly became more indistinct as the wind drove to the place the rain of ashes, which spread over them, first like a grey gauze veil, then extinguished the last glimpse of her face, and soon, like a northern winter snowfall, buried the whole figure under a smooth cover. Outside, the pillars of the Temple of Apollo rose—now, however, only half of them, for the grey fall of ashes heaped itself likewise against them.

When Norbert Hanold awoke, he still heard the confused cries of the Pompeiians who were seeking safety, and the dully resounding boom of the surf of the turbulent sea. Then he came to his senses; the sun cast a golden gleam of light across his bed; it was an April morning and outside sounded the various noises of the city, cries of vendors, and the rumbling of vehicles. Yet the dream picture still stood most distinctly in every detail before his open eyes, and some time was necessary before he could get rid of a feeling that he had really been present at the destruction on the bay of Naples, that night nearly two thousand years ago. While he was dressing, he first became gradually free from it; yet he did not succeed, even by the use of critical thought, in breaking away from the idea that Gradiva had lived in Pompeii and had been buried there in 79 A.D. Rather, the former conjecture had now become to him an established certainty and now the second also was added. With woeful feeling he now viewed in his living room the old relief, which had assumed new significance for him. It was, in a way, a tombstone by which the artist had preserved for posterity the likeness of the girl who had so early departed this life. Yet if one looked at her with enlightened understanding, the expression of her whole being left no doubt that, on that fateful night, she had actually lain down to die with just such calm as the dream had showed. An old proverb says that the darlings of the gods are taken from the earth in the full vigor of youth.

Without having yet put on a collar, in morning attire, with slippers on his feet, Norbert leaned on the open window and gazed out. The spring, which had finally arrived in the north also, was without, but announced itself in the great quarry of the city only by the blue sky and the soft air. Yet a foreboding of it reached the senses, and awoke in remote, sunny places a desire for leaf-green, fragrance, and bird song; a breath of it came as far as this place; the market women on the street had their baskets adorned with a few bright wildflowers, and at an open window a canary in a cage warbled his song. Norbert felt sorry for the poor fellow, for, beneath the clear tone, in spite of the joyful note, he heard the longing for freedom and the open.

Yet the thoughts of the young archaeologist dallied but briefly there, for something else had crowded into them. Not until then had he become aware that in the dream he had not noticed exactly whether the living Gradiva had really walked as the piece of sculpture represented her, and as the women of today, at any rate, did not walk. That was remarkable because it was the basis of his scientific interest in the relief; on the other hand, it could be explained by his excitement over the danger to her life. He tried, in vain, however, to recall her gait.

Then suddenly something like a thrill passed through him; in the first moment he could not say whence. But then his sense of reality returned. Down in the street, with her back toward him, a female, from figure and dress undoubtedly a young lady, was walking along with easy, elastic step. Her dress, which reached only to her ankles, she held lifted a little in her left hand, and he saw that in walking the sole of her slender foot, as it followed, rose for a moment vertically on the tips of the toes. It appeared so, but the distance and the fact that he was looking down did not admit of certainty.

Quickly Norbert Hanold was in the street without knowing exactly how he had come there. He had, like a boy sliding down a railing, flown like lightning down the steps, and was running down among the carriages, carts, and people. The latter directed looks of wonder at him, and from several lips came laughing, half-mocking exclamations. He was unaware that these referred to him. His glance was seeking the young lady and he thought that he distinguished her dress a few dozen steps ahead of him, but only the upper part; of the lower half, and of her feet, he could perceive nothing, for they were concealed by the crowd thronging on the sidewalk.

Now an old comfortable vegetable woman stretched her hand toward his sleeve, stopped him and said, half grinning, "Say, my dear, you probably drank a little too much last night, and are you looking for your bed here in the street? You would do better to go home and look at yourself in the mirror."

A burst of laughter from those nearby proved it true that he had shown himself in garb not suited to public appearance, and brought him now to the realization that he had heedlessly run from his room. This surprised him because he insisted upon conventionality of attire. Forsaking his project, he quickly returned home—apparently, however, with his mind still somewhat confused by the dream and dazed by illusion, for he had perceived that, at the laughter and exclamation, the young lady had turned her head a moment and he thought he had seen not the face of a stranger, but that of Gradiva looking down upon him.

Because of considerable property, Dr. Norbert Hanold was in the pleasant position of being unhampered master of his own acts and wishes and, upon the appearance of any inclination, of not depending for expert counsel about it on any higher court than his own decision. In this way he differed most favorably from the canary, who could only warble out, without success, his inborn impulse to get out of the cage into the sunny open. Otherwise, however, the young archaeologist resembled the latter in many respects. He had not come into the world and grown up in natural freedom, but already at birth had been hedged in by the grating with which family tradition, by education and pre-destination, had surrounded him. From his early childhood no doubt had existed in his parents' house that he, as the only son of a university professor and antiquarian, was called upon to preserve, if possible to exalt, by that very activity the glory of his father's name; so this business continuity had always seemed to him the natural task of his future. He had clung loyally to it even after the early deaths of his parents had left him absolutely alone; in connection with his brilliantly passed examination in philology, he had taken the prescribed student trip to Italy and had seen in the original a number of old works of art whose imitations only had formerly been acessible to him. Nothing more instructive for him than the collections of Florence, Rome,

Naples could be offered anywhere; he could furnish evidence
that the period of his stay there had been used excellently
for the enrichment of his knowledge, and he had returned
home fully satisfied to devote himself with the new acquisi-
tions to his science.

That, besides these objects from the distant past, the
present still existed round about him, he felt only in the
most shadowy way; for his feelings marble and bronze were
not dead, but rather the only really vital thing which expressed the purpose and value of human life; and so he sat
in the midst of his walls, books, and pictures, with no need
of any other intercourse, but whenever possible avoiding
the latter as an empty squandering of time and only very
reluctantly submitting occasionally to an inevitable party,
attendance at which was required by the connections handed
down from his parents. Yet it was known that at such gather-
ings he was present without eyes or ears for his surroundings,
and, as soon as it was any way permissible, he always took
his leave, under some pretext, at the end of the lunch or
dinner; and on the street he greeted none of those whom
he had sat with at the table. That served, especially with
young ladies, to put him in a rather unfavorable light; for
upon meeting even a girl with whom he had, by way of
exception, spoken a few words, he looked at her without a
greeting as at a quite unknown person whom he had never
seen.

Although perhaps archaeology, in itself, might be a rather
curious science and although its alloy had effected a remarkable amalgamation with Norbert Hanold's nature, it could
not exercise much attraction for others and afforded even
him little enjoyment in life according to the usual views of

youth. Yet, with perhaps kind intent, nature had put into his blood, without his knowing of the possession, a thoroughly unscientific sort of corrective, a most lively imagination, which was able to find expression not only in his dreams, but also in his waking life, and essentially made his mind not preponderantly adapted to strict research method devoid of interest. From this endowment, however, originated another similarity between him and the canary. The latter was born in captivity and had never known anything else than the cage which confined him in narrow quarters; but he had an inner feeling that something was lacking to him and sounded from his throat his desire for the unknown. Thus Norbert Hanold understood it, pitied him for it, returned to his room, leaned again from the window and was thereupon moved by a feeling that he, too, lacked a nameless something. Meditation on it, therefore, could be of no use. The indefinite stir of emotion came from the mild spring air, the sunbeams and the broad expanse with its fragrant breath, and formed a comparison for him; he was likewise sitting in a cage behind a grating. Yet this idea was immediately followed by the palliating one that his position was more advantageous than that of the canary, for he had in his possession wings which were hindered by nothing from flying out into the open at his pleasure.

But that was an idea which developed more upon reflection. Norbert gave himself up for a time to this occupation; yet it was not long before the project of a spring journey assumed definite shape. This he carried out that very day; he packed a light valise, and, before he went south by the night express, cast at nightfall another regretful departing glance on Gradiva, who, steeped in the last rays of the sun, seemed to step out with more buoyancy than ever over the invisible steppingstones beneath her feet. Even if the impulse for travel had originated in a nameless feeling, further reflection had, however, granted, as a matter of course, that it must serve a scientific purpose. It had occurred to him that he had neglected to inform himself with accuracy about some important archaeological questions in connection with some statues in Rome and, without stopping on the way, he made the journey of a day and a half thither.

Not very many personally experience the beauty of going from Germany to Italy in the spring when one is young, wealthy, and independent, for even those endowed with the three latter requirements are not always accessible to such a feeling for beauty, especially if they (and, alas, they form the majority) are in couples on the days or weeks after a wedding. For these allow nothing to pass without an extraordinary delight, which is expressed in numerous superlatives; and finally they bring back home, as profit, only what they would have discovered, felt, or enjoyed exactly as much by staying there. In the spring such dualists usually swarm over the Alpine passes in exactly opposite direction to the birds of passage. During the whole journey they billed and cooed around Norbert as if they were in a rolling dovecot, and for the first time in his life he was compelled to observe his fellow beings more closely with eye and ear. Although, from their speech, they were all his German countrymen, his racial identity with them awoke in him no feeling of pride, but the rather opposite one—that he had done reasonably well to bother as little as possible with the *homo sapiens* of Linnaean classification, especially in connection with the feminine half of this species. For the first time he saw also, in his immediate vicinity, people brought together by the mating impulse without his being able to understand what had been the mutual cause. It remained incomprehensible to him why the women had chosen these men, and still more perplexing why the choice of the men had fallen upon these women. Every time he raised his eyes, his glance had to fall on the face of some one of them and it found none which charmed the eye by outer attraction or possessed indication of intellect or good nature. To be sure, he lacked a standard for measuring, for of course one could not compare the women of today with the sublime beauty of the old works of art; yet he had a dark suspicion that he was not to blame for this unkind view, but that in all expressions there was something lacking which ordinary life was in duty bound to offer. So he reflected for many hours on the strange impulses of human beings, and came to the conclusion that of all their follies, marriage, at any rate, took the prize as the greatest and most incomprehensible one, and the senseless wedding trips to Italy somehow capped the climax of this buffoonery.

Again, however, he was reminded of the canary that he had left behind in captivity, for he also sat here in a cage, cooped in by the faces of young bridal couples which were as rapturous as vapid, past which his glance could only occasionally stray through the window. Therefore it can be easily explained that the things passing outside before his eyes made other impressions on him than when he had seen them some years before. The olive foliage had more of a silver sheen; the solitary, towering cypresses and pines here and there were delineated with more beautiful and more distinctive outlines; the places situated on the mountain heights seemed to him more charming, as if each one, in a manner, were an individual with different expression; and Lake Trasimeno seemed to him of a soft blue such as he had never noticed in any surface of water. He had a feeling that a nature unknown to him was surrounding the railway tracks, as if he must have passed through these places before in continual twilight, or during a grey rainfall, and was now seeing them for the first time in their golden abundance of color. A few times he surprised himself in a desire, formerly unknown to him, to alight and seek afoot the way to this or that place because it looked to him as if it might be concealing something peculiar or mysterious. Yet he did not allow himself to be misled by such unreasonable impulses, but the *diretissimo* took him directly to Rome where, already, before the entrance into the station, the ancient world with the ruins of the temple of Minerva Medica received him. When he had finally freed himself from his cage filled with "inseparables," he immediately secured accommodations in a hotel well known to him, in order to look about from there, without excessive haste, for a private house satisfactory to him.

Such a one he had not yet found in the course of the next day, but returned to his *albergo* again in the evening and went to sleep rather exhausted by the unaccustomed Italian air, the strong sun, much wandering about and the noise of the streets. Soon consciousness began to fade, but just as he was about to fall asleep he was again awakened, for his room was connected with the adjoining one by a door concealed only by a wardrobe, and into the next room came two guests, who had taken possession of it that morning. From the voices which sounded through the thin partition, they were a man and a woman who unmistakably belonged to that class of German spring birds of passage with whom he had yesterday journeyed hither from Florence. Their frame of mind seemed to give decidedly favorable testimony concerning the hotel cuisine, and it might be due to the good quality of a Castellin-Romani wine that they exchanged ideas and feelings most distinctly and audibly in the North German tongue:

"My only Augustus."

"My sweet Gretchen."

"Now again we have each other."

"Yes, at last we are alone again."

"Must we do more sight-seeing tomorrow?"

"At breakfast we shall look in Baedeker for what is still to be done."

"My only Augustus, to me you are much more pleasing than Apollo Belvedere."

"And I have often thought, my sweet Gretchen, that you are much more beautiful than the Capitoline Venus."

"Is the volcano that we want to climb near here?"

"No, I think we'll have to ride a few hours more in the train to get there."

"If it should begin to belch flame just as we got to the middle, what would you do?"

"Then my only thought would be to save you, and I would take you in my arms—so."

"Don't scratch yourself on that pin!"

"I can think of nothing more beautiful than to shed my blood for you."

"My only Augustus."

"My sweet Gretchen."

With that the conversation ceased, Norbert heard another ill-defined rustling and moving of chairs, then it became quiet and he fell back into a doze which transported him to Pompeii just as Vesuvius again began its eruption. A vivid throng of fleeing people caught him, and among them he saw Apollo Belvedere lift up the Capitoline Venus, take her away and place her safely upon some object in a dark shadow; it seemed to be a carriage or cart on which she was to be carried off, for a rattling sound was soon heard from that direction. This mythological occurrence did not amaze the young archaeologist, but it struck him as remarkable that the two talked German, not Greek, to each other for, as they half regained their senses, he heard them say:

"My sweet Gretchen."

"My only Augustus."

But after that the dream-picture changed completely. Absolute silence took the place of the confused sound, and instead of smoke and the glow of fire, bright, hot sunlight rested on the ruins of the buried city. This likewise changed gradually, became a bed on whose white linen golden beams circled up to his eyes, and Norbert Hanold awoke in the scintillating spring morning of Rome.

Within him, also, however, something had changed; he could not surmise why but a strangely oppressive feeling had again taken possession of him, a feeling that he was imprisoned in a cage which this time was called Rome. As he opened the window, there screamed up from the street dozens of vendors' cries far more shrill to his ear than those in his German home. He had come only from one noisy quarry to another, and a strangely uncanny horror of antique collections—of meeting there Apollo Belvedere or the Capitoline Venus—frightened him away. Thus, after brief consideration, he refrained from his intention of looking for a dwelling, hastily packed his valise again and went farther south by train. To escape the "inseparables," he did this in a third-class coach, expecting at the same time to find there an interesting and scientifically useful company of Italian folk-types, the former models of antique works of art. Yet he found nothing but the usual dirt, Monopol cigars which smelled horrible, little warped fellows beating about with arms and legs, and members of the female sex, in contrast to whom his coupled countrywomen seemed to his memory almost like Olympian goddesses.

Two days later Norbert Hanold occupied a rather questionable space called a "room" in Hotel Diomede beside the eucalyptus-guarded *ingresso* to the excavations of Pompeii. He had intended to stay in Naples for some time to study again more closely the sculptures and wall-paintings in the Museo Nazionale, but he had had an experience there similar to that in Rome. In the room for the collection of Pompeiian household furniture he found himself surrounded by a cloud of feminine, ultra-fashionable travel costumes, which had doubtless all quickly replaced the virgin radiance of satin, silk, or lace bridal finery; each one clung to the arm of a young or old companion, likewise faultlessly attired, according to men's fashion standards. Norbert's newly gained insight into a field of knowledge formerly unknown to him had advanced so far as to permit him to recognize them at first glance: every man was Augustus, every girl was Gretchen. Only this came to light here by means of other forms of conversation tempered, moderated, and modified by the ear of publicity.

"Oh, look, that was practical of them; we'll surely have to get a meat warmer like that too."

"Yes, but for the food that my wife cooks it must be made of silver."

"How do you know that what I cook will taste so good to you?"

The question was accompanied by a roguish, arch glance and was answered in the affirmative, with a glance varnished with lacquer, "What you serve to me can be nothing but delicious."

"No; that surely is a thimble! Did the people of those days have needles?"

"It almost seems so, but you could not have done anything with that, my darling; it would be much too large even for your thumb."

"Do you really think that? And do you like slender fingers better than broad ones?"

"Yours I do not need to see; by touch I could discover them, in the deepest darkness, among all the others in the world."

"That is really awfully interesting. Do we still really have to go to Pompeii also?"

"No, that will hardly pay. There are only old stones and rubbish there; whatever was of value, Baedeker says, was brought here. I fear the sun there would be too hot for your delicate complexion, and I could never forgive myself that."

"What if you should suddenly have a negress for a wife?"

"No, my imagination fortunately does not reach that far, but a freckle on your little nose would make me unhappy.

I think, if it is agreeable to you, we'll go to Capri tomorrow, my dear. There everything is said to be very comfortable and in the wonderful light of the Blue Grotto I shall first realize completely what a great prize I have drawn in the lottery of happiness."

"You—if any one hears that, I shall be almost ashamed. But wherever you take me, it is agreeable to me, and makes no difference, for I have you with me."

Augustus and Gretchen over again, somewhat toned down and tempered for eye and ear. It seemed to Norbert Hanold that he had had thin honey poured upon him from all sides and that he had to dispose of it swallow by swallow. A sick feeling came over him and he ran out of the Museo Nazionale to the nearest *osteria* to drink a glass of vermouth. Again and again the thought intruded itself upon his mind: Why did these couples by the hundred fill the museums of Florence, Rome, Naples, instead of devoting themselves to their plural occupations in their native Germany? Yet from a number of chats and tender talks, it seemed to him that the majority of these bird-couples did not intend to nest in the rubbish of Pompeii, but considered a side trip to Capri much more profitable; and thence originated his sudden impulse to do what they did not do. There was at any rate offered to him a chance to be freed from the main flock of this migration and to find what he was vainly seeking here in Italy. That was also a pair, not a wedding couple, but two members of the same family without cooing bills—silence and science, two calm sisters who were the only ones that could be counted upon for satisfactory shelter. His desire for them contained something formerly unknown to him; if it had not been a contradiction in itself, he

could have applied to this impulse the epithet "passionate"
—and an hour later he was already sitting in a *carrozella*
which bore him through the interminable Portici and Resina.

The journey was like one through a street splendidly
adorned for an old Roman victor. To the right and left almost every house spread out to dry in the sun, like yellow
tapestry hangings, a superabundant wealth of *pasta di
Napoli,* the greatest delicacy of the country, thick or thin
macaroni, vermicelli, spaghetti, canelloni, and fidelini, to
which the smoke of fats from cook-shops, dust-clouds, flies
and fleas, the fish scales flying about in the air, chimney
smoke and other day and night influences lent the familiar
delicacy of their taste. Then the cone of Vesuvius looked
down close by across brown lava fields; at the right extended
the gulf of shimmering blue, as if composed of liquid malachite and lapis lazuli. The little nutshell on wheels flew, as
if whirled forth by a mad storm and as if every moment
must be its last, over the dreadful pavement of Torre del
Greco, rattled through Torre dell'Annunziata, reached the
Dioscuri, Hotel Suisse and Hotel Diomede, which measured
their power of attraction in a ceaseless, silent, but ferocious
struggle, and stopped before the latter, whose classic name
again, as on his first visit, had determined the choice of the
young archaeologist. With apparently, at least, the greatest
composure, however, the modern Swiss competitor viewed
this event before its very door. It was calm because no different water from what it used was boiled in the pots of its
classic neighbor; and the antique splendors temptingly displayed for sale over there had not come to light again after
two thousand years under the ashes, any more than the ones
which it had.

Thus Norbert Hanold, contrary to all expectations and intentions, had been transported in a few days from northern Germany to Pompeii. He found the Diomede not too much filled with human guests, but on the other hand populously inhabited by the *musca domestica communis,* the common housefly. He had never been subject to violent emotions; yet a hatred of these two-winged creatures burned within him. He considered them the basest evil invention of nature, on their account much preferred the winter to the summer as the only time suited to human life, and recognized in them invincible proof against the existence of a rational world-system. Now they received him here several months earlier than he would have fallen to their infamy in Germany, rushed immediately about him in dozens, as upon a victim patiently awaited, whizzed before his eyes, buzzed in his ears, tangled themselves in his hair, tickled his nose, forehead, and hands. Therein many reminded him of honeymoon couples; probably they were also saying to each other in their language, "My only Augustus" and "My sweet Gretchen."

In the mind of the tormented man rose a longing for a *scacciamosche,* a splendidly made fly-swatter like one unearthed from a burial vault, which he had seen in the Etruscan museum in Bologna. Thus, in antiquity, this worthless creature had likewise been the scourge of humanity, more vicious and more inevitable than scorpions, venomous snakes, tigers, and sharks, which were bent upon only physical injury, rending or devouring the ones attacked; against the former one could guard himself by thoughtful conduct. From the common housefly, however, there was no protection, and it paralyzed, disturbed, and finally shat-

tered the psychic life of human beings, their capacity for
thinking and working, every lofty flight of imagination, and
every beautiful feeling. Hunger or thirst for blood did not
impel them, but solely the diabolical desire to torture; it
was the *Ding an sich* in which absolute evil had found its
incarnation. The Etruscan *scacciamosche,* a wooden handle
with a bunch of fine leather strips fastened to it, proved the
following: flies had destroyed the most exalted poetic
thoughts in the mind of Aeschylus; they had caused the
chisel of Phidias to make an irremediable slip, had run over
the brow of Zeus, the breast of Aphrodite, and from head
to foot of all Olympian gods and goddesses; and Norbert
felt in his soul that the service of a human being was to be
estimated, above all, according to the number of flies he
had killed, pierced, burned up, or exterminated in hecatombs
during his life, as avenger of his whole race from remotest
antiquity.

For the achievement of such fame, he lacked here the
necessary weapon, and like the greatest battle hero of antiquity, who had, however, been alone and unable to do
otherwise, he left the field, or rather his room, in view of
the hundredfold overwhelming number of the common foe.
Outside it dawned upon him that he had thereby done in a
small way what he would have to repeat on a larger scale on
the morrow. Pompeii, too, apparently offered no peacefully
gratifying abode for his needs. To this idea was added, at
least dimly, another—that his dissatisfaction was probably
not caused by his surroundings alone, but to a degree had
its origin in him. To be sure, flies had always been very
repulsive to him, but they had never before transported him
into such raging fury as this. On account of the journey his

nerves were undeniably in an excited and irritable condition, for which indoor air and overwork at home during the
winter had probably begun to pave the way. He felt that
he was out of sorts because he lacked something without
being able to explain what, and this ill-humor he took everywhere with him; of course flies and bridal couples swarming
*en masse* were not calculated to make life agreeable anywhere. Yet if he did not wish to wrap himself in a thick
cloud of self-righteousness, it could not remain concealed
from him that he was traveling around Italy just as aimless,
senseless, blind, and deaf as they, but with considerably less
capacity for enjoyment. For his traveling companion, science, had, most decidedly, much of an old Trappist about
her; she did not open her mouth when she was not spoken
to, and it seemed to him that he was almost forgetting in
what language he had communed with her.

It was now too late in the day to go into Pompeii through
the *ingresso*. Norbert remembered a circuit he had once
made on the old city wall, and he attempted to mount the
latter by means of all sorts of bushes and wild growth. Thus
he wandered along for some distance a little above the city
of graves, which lay on his right, motionless and quiet. It
looked like a dead rubbish field already almost covered with
shadow, for the evening sun stood in the west not far from
the edge of the Tyrrhenian Sea. Round about on the other
hand it still bathed all the hilltops and fields with an en-
chanting brilliancy of life, gilded the smoke-cone rising
above the Vesuvius crater, and clad the peaks and pinnacles
of Monte Sant' Angelo in purple. High and solitary rose
Monte Epomeo from the sparkling blue sea glittering with
golden light, from which Cape Miseno reared itself with

dark outline, like a mysterious, titanic structure. Wherever the gaze rested, a wonderful picture was spread, combining charm and sublimity, remote past and joyous present. Norbert Hanold had expected to find here what he vaguely longed for. Yet he was not in the mood for it, although no bridal couples or flies molested him on the deserted wall; even nature was unable to offer him what he lacked in his surroundings and within himself. With a calmness bordering closely on indifference, he let his eyes pass over the all-pervading beauty, and did not regret in the least that it was growing pale and fading away in the sunset, but returned to the Diomede, as he had come, dissatisfied.

But as he had now, although with ill success, been conveyed to this place through his indiscretion, he reached the decision overnight to get from the folly he had committed at least one day of scientific profit; and he went to Pompeii on the regular road as soon as the *ingresso* was opened in the morning. In little groups commanded by official guides, armed with red Baedekers or their foreign cousins, longing for secret excavations of their own, there wandered before and behind him the population of the two hotels. The still-fresh morning air was filled almost exclusively by English or Anglo-American chatter; the German couples were making each other mutually happy with German sweets and inspiration up there on Capri behind Monte Sant' Angelo at the breakfast table of the Pagano.

Norbert remembered how to free himself soon, by well chosen words, combined with a good *mancia*, from the burden of a *guida* and was able to pursue his purposes alone and unhindered. It afforded him some satisfaction to know

that he possessed a faultless memory; wherever his glance
rested, everything lay and stood exactly as he remembered
it, as if only yesterday he had imprinted it in his mind by
means of expert observation. This continually repeated experience brought, however, the added feeling that his presence there seemed really very unnecessary, and a decided indifference took possession of his eyes and his intellect more
and more, as during the evening on the wall. Although, when
he looked up, the pine-shaped smoke-cone of Vesuvius generally stood before him against the blue sky, yet, strangely
enough, he did not even once remember that he had
dreamed some time ago that he had been present at the
destruction of Pompeii by the volcanic eruption of 79.
Wandering around for hours made him tired and half-sleepy,
of course; yet he felt not the least suggestion of anything
dreamlike. But there lay about him only a confusion of
fragments of ancient gate arches, pillars, and walls significant to the highest degree for archaeology, but, viewed without the esoteric aid of this science, really not much else than
a big pile of rubbish, neatly arranged, to be sure, but extremely devoid of interest; and although science and dreams
were wont formerly to stand on footings exactly opposed,
they had apparently here today come to an agreement to
withdraw their aid from Norbert Hanold and deliver him
over absolutely to the aimlessness of his walking and standing around.

So he had wandered in all directions from the Forum to
the Amphitheater, from the Porta di Stabia to the Porta del
Vesuvio through the Street of Tombs, as well as through
countless others; and the sun had likewise, in the meanwhile, made its accustomed morning journey to the position

where it usually changes to the more comfortable descent toward the sea. Thereby, to the great satisfaction of their misunderstood, hoarsely eloquent guides, it gave the English and American men and women, forced to go there by a traveler's sense of duty, a signal to become mindful of the superior comfort of sitting at the lunch-tables of the twin hotels; besides they had seen with their own eyes everything that could be required for conversation on the other side of the ocean and channel. So the separate groups, satiated by the past, started on the return, ebbed in common movement down through the Via Marina, in order not to lose meals at the, to be sure somewhat euphemistically Lucullan, tables of the present, in the house of Diomede or of Mr. Swiss. In consideration of all the outer and inner circumstances, this was doubtless also the wisest thing that they could do —for the noon sun of May was decidedly well disposed toward the lizards, butterflies, and other winged inhabitants or visitors of the extensive mass of ruins, but for the northern complexion of a madame or miss its perpendicular obtrusiveness was unquestionably beginning to become less kindly. And, supposedly in some causal connection with this, the "charmings" had already in the last hour considerably diminished, the "shockings" had increased in the same proportion, and the masculine "ah's" proceeding from rows of teeth even more widely distended than before had begun a noticeable transition to yawning.

It was remarkable, however, that simultaneously with their vanishing, what had formerly been the city of Pompeii assumed an entirely changed appearance, but not a living one; it now appeared rather to be becoming completely petrified in dead immobility. Yet out of it stirred a feeling that death was beginning to talk, although not in a manner intelligible to human ears. To be sure, here and there was a sound as if a whisper were proceeding from the stone which, however, only the softly murmuring south wind, Atabulus, awoke—he who, two thousand years ago, had buzzed in this fashion about the temples, halls and houses, and was now carrying on his playful game with the green, shimmering stalks on the low ruins. From the coast of Africa he often rushed across, casting forth wild, full blasts; he was not doing that today, but was gently fanning again the old acquaintances which had come to light again. He could not, however, refrain from his natural tendency to devastate, and blew with hot breath, even though lightly, on everything that he encountered on the way.

In this, the sun, his eternally youthful mother, helped him. She strengthened his fiery breath, and accomplished, besides, what he could not, steeped everything with trembling, glittering, dazzling splendor. As with a golden eraser, she effaced from the edges of the houses on the *semitae* and *crepidine viarum,* as the sidewalks were once called, every slight shadow, cast into all the vestibules, inner courts, peristyles, and balconies her luminous radiance, or desultory rays where a shelter blocked her direct approach. Hardly anywhere was there a nook which successfully protected itself against the ocean of light and veiled itself in a dusky, silver web; every street lay between the old walls like long, rippling, white strips of linen spread out to bleach; and without exception all were equally motionless and mute, for not only had the last of the rasping and nasal tones of the English and American messengers disappeared, but the former slight evidences of lizard-life and butterfly-life seemed also to have left the silent city of ruins. They had not really done so, but the gaze perceived no more movement from them. As had been the custom of their ancestors out on the mountain slopes and cliff walls, for thousands of years, when the great Pan laid himself to sleep, here, too, in order not to disturb him, they had stretched themselves out motionless or, folding their wings, had squatted here and there. And it seemed as if, in this place, they felt even more strongly the command of the hot, holy, noonday quiet in whose ghostly hour life must be silent and suppressed, because during it the dead awake and begin to talk in toneless spirit-language.

This changed aspect which the things round about had assumed really thrust itself less upon the vision than it aroused the emotions, or, more correctly, an unnamed sixth sense; this latter, however, was stimulated so strongly and persistently that a person endowed with it could not throw off the effect produced upon him. To be sure, of those estimable boarders already busy with their soup spoons at the two *alberghi* near the *ingresso*, hardly a man or woman would have been counted among those thus invested; but nature had once bestowed this great attention upon Norbert Hanold, and he had to submit to its effects—not at all because he had an understanding with it, however, for he wished nothing at all and desired nothing more than that he might be sitting quietly in his study with an instructive book in his hand, instead of having undertaken this aimless spring journey. Yet as he had turned back from the Street of Tombs through the gate of Hercules into the center of the city and at Casa di Sallustio had turned to the left, quite without purpose or thought, into the narrow *vicolo*, suddenly

that sixth sense was awakened in him. But this last expression was not really fitting; rather he was transported by it
into a strangely dreamy condition, about halfway between
a waking state and loss of senses. As if guarding a secret,
everywhere round about him, suffused in light, lay deathly
silence, so breathless that even his own lungs hardly dared
to take in air.

He stood at the intersection of two streets where the
Vicolo Mercurio crossed the broader Strada di Mercurio,
which stretched out to right and left. In answer to the god
of commerce, business and trades had formerly had their
abodes here; the street corners spoke silently of it; many
shops with broken counters, inlaid with marble, opened
out upon them; here the arrangement indicated a bakery,
there a number of large, convex, earthenware jugs indicated
an oil or flour business. Opposite more slender, two-handled
jars set into the counters showed that the space behind them
had been a barroom; surely, in the evening, slaves and maids
of the neighborhood might have thronged here to get wine
for their masters in their own jugs; one could see that the
now illegible inscription inlaid with mosaic on the sidewalk
in front of the shop was worn by many feet; probably it had
held out to passers-by a recommendation of the excellent
wine. On the outer wall, at about half the height of a man,
was visible a graffito probably scratched into the plastering,
with his fingernail or an iron nail, by a schoolboy, perhaps
derisively explaining the praise in this way, that the owner's
wine owed its peerlessness to a generous addition of water.
For from the scratch there seemed raised before Norbert
Hanold's eyes the word *caupo*—or was it an illusion? Certainly he could not settle it. He possessed a certain skill in

deciphering graffiti which were difficult, and had already accomplished widely recognized work in that field; yet at this time his skill completely failed him. Not only that: he had a feeling that he did not understand any Latin, and it was absurd of him to wish to read what a Pompeiian school youth had scratched into the wall two thousand years before.

Not only had all his science left him, but it had left him without the least desire to regain it; he remembered it as from a great distance, and he felt that it had been like an old, dried-up, boring aunt, the dullest and most superfluous creature in the world. What she uttered with puckered lips and sapient mien, and presented as wisdom, was all vain, empty pompousness, and merely gnawed at the dry rind of the fruit of knowledge without revealing anything of its content, the germ of life, or bringing anything to the point of inner, intelligent enjoyment. What it taught was a lifeless, archaeological view, and what came from its mouth was a dead, philological language. These helped in no way to a comprehension with soul, mind, and heart, or whatever one wanted to call it; instead, anyone who harbored a desire for such a comprehension had to stand here alone, among the remains of the past, the only living person in the hot noonday silence, in order not to see with physical eyes nor hear with corporeal ears. Then something came forth everywhere without movement and a soundless speech began; then the sun dissolved the tomb-like rigidity of the old stones, a glowing thrill passed through them, the dead awoke, and Pompeii began to live again.

The thoughts in Norbert Hanold's mind were not really blasphemous, but he had an indefinite feeling deserving of that adjective; and with this, standing motionless, he looked before him down the Strada di Mercurio toward the city wall. The angular lava-blocks of its pavement still lay as faultlessly fitted together as before the devastation, and each one was of a light-grey color; yet such dazzling luster brooded over them that they stretched like a quilted silver-white ribbon passing in faintly glowing void between the silent walls and by the side of column fragments.

Then suddenly—

With open eyes he gazed along the street, yet it seemed to him as if he were doing it in a dream. A little to the right something suddenly stepped forth from the Casa di Castore e Polluce, and across the lava steppingstones, which led from the house to the other side of the Strada di Mercurio, Gradiva stepped buoyantly.

Quite indubitably it was she; even if the sunbeams did surround her figure as with a thin veil of gold, he perceived her in profile as plainly and as distinctly as on the bas-relief. Her head, whose crown was entwined with a scarf which fell to her neck, inclined forward a little; her left hand held up lightly the extremely voluminous dress and, as it reached only to her ankles, one could perceive clearly that in advancing, the right foot, lingering, if only for a moment, rose on the tips of the toes almost perpendicularly. Here, however, it was not a stone representation, everything in uniform colorlessness; the dress, apparently made of extremely soft, clinging material, was not of cold marble-white, but of a warm tone verging faintly on yellow, and her hair, wavy under the scarf on her brow, and peeping forth at the temples, stood out, with golden-brown radiance, in bold contrast to her alabaster countenance.

As soon as he caught sight of her, Norbert's memory was

clearly awakened to the fact that he had seen her here once already in a dream, walking thus, the night that she had lain down as if to sleep over there in the Forum on the steps of the Temple of Apollo. With this memory he became conscious, for the first time, of something else; he had, without himself knowing the motive in his heart, come to Italy on that account, and had, without stop, continued from Rome and Naples to Pompeii to see if he could here find trace of her (and that in a literal sense), for, with her unusual gait, she must have left behind in the ashes a footprint different from all the others.

Again it was a noonday dream-picture that passed there before him and yet also a reality. For that was apparent from an effect which it produced. On the last steppingstone on the farther side, there lay stretched out motionless, in the burning sunlight, a big lizard, whose body, as if woven of gold and malachite, glistened brightly to Norbert's eyes. Before the approaching foot, however, it darted down suddenly and wriggled away over the white, gleaming lava pavement.

Gradiva crossed the steppingstones with her calm buoyancy, and now, turning her back, walked along on the opposite sidewalk; her destination seemed to be the house of Adonis. Before it she stopped a moment, too, but passed then, as if after further deliberation, down farther through the Strada di Mercurio. On the left, of the more elegant buildings, there now stood only the Casa di Apollo, named after the numerous representations of Apollo excavated there, and, to the man who was gazing after her, it seemed again that she had also surely chosen the portico of the Temple of Apollo for her death sleep. Probably she was closely associated with the cult of the sun-god and was going there. Soon, however, she stopped again; steppingstones crossed the street here, too, and she walked back again to the right side. Thus she turned the other side of her face toward him and looked a little different, for her left hand, which held up her gown, was not visible and instead of her curved arm, the right one hung down straight. At a greater distance now, however, the golden waves of sunlight floated around her with a thicker web of veiling, and did not allow him to distinguish where she had stopped, for she disappeared suddenly before the house of Meleager. Norbert Hanold still stood without having moved a limb. With his eyes, and this time with his corporeal ones, he had surveyed, step by step, her vanishing form. Now, at length, he drew a deep breath, for his breast too had remained almost motionless.

Simultaneously the sixth sense, suppressing the others completely, held him absolutely in its sway. Had what had just stood before him been a product of his imagination or a reality?

He did not know that, nor whether he was awake or dreaming, and tried in vain to collect his thoughts. Then, however, a strange shudder passed down his spine. He saw and heard nothing, yet he felt from the secret inner vibratons that Pompeii had begun to live about him in the noonday hour of spirits, and so Gradiva lived again, too, and had gone into the house which she had occupied before the fateful August day of the year 79.

From his former visit he was acquainted with the Casa di Meleagro. He had not yet gone there this time, however, but had merely stopped briefly in the Museo Nazionale of Naples before the wall paintings of Meleager and his Arcadian huntress companion, Atalanta, which had been found in the Strada di Mercurio in that house, and after which the latter had been named. Yet as he now again acquired the ability to move and walked toward it, he began to doubt whether it really bore its name after the slayer of the Caledonian boar. He suddenly recalled a Greek poet, Meleager, who, to be sure, had probably lived about a century before the destruction of Pompeii. A descendant of his, however, might have come here and built the house for himself. That agreed with something else that had awakened in his memory, for he remembered his supposition, or rather a definite conviction, that Gradiva had been of Greek descent. To be sure there mingled with his idea the figure of Atalanta as Ovid had pictured it in his *Metamorphoses*:

> . . . her floating vest
> A polished buckle clasped—her careless locks
> In simple knot were gathered . . .*

He could not recall the verses word for word, but their content was present in his mind; and from his store of knowledge was added the fact that Cleopatra was the name of the young wife of Oeneus' son, Meleager. More probably this had nothing to do with him, but with the Greek poet, Meleager. Thus, under the glowing sun of the Campagna, there was a mythological-literary-historical-archaeological juggling in his head.

When he had passed the house of Castor and Pollux and that of the Centaur, he stood before the Casa di Meleagro, from whose threshold there looked up at him, still discernible, the inlaid greeting "Ave." On the wall of the vestibule, Mercury was handing Fortuna a pouch filled with money;

* Translation by Henry King.

that probably indicated, allegorically, the riches and other fortunate circumstances of the former dweller. Behind this opened up the inner court, the center of which was occupied by a marble table supported by three griffins.

Empty and silent, the room lay there, appearing absolutely unfamiliar to the man, as he entered, awaking no memory that he had already been here; yet he then recalled it, for the interior of the house offered a deviation from that of the other excavated buildings of the city. The peristyle adjoined the inner court on the other side of the balcony toward the rear—not in the usual way, but at the left side. It was therefore of greater extent and more splendid appearance than any other in Pompeii. It was framed by a colonnade supported by two dozen pillars painted red on the lower, and white on the upper, half. These lent solemnity to the great silent space; here in the center was a spring with a beautifully wrought enclosure, which served as a fishpool. Apparently the house must have been the dwelling of an estimable man of culture and artistic sense.

Norbert's gaze passed around, and he listened. Yet nowhere about did anything stir, nor was the slightest sound audible. Amidst this cold stone there was no longer a breath; if Gradiva had gone into the house of Meleager, she had already dissolved again into nothing. At the rear of the peristyle was another room, an *oecus*, the former dining room, likewise surrounded on three sides by pillars painted yellow, which shimmered from a distance in the light, as if they were encrusted with gold. Between them, however, shone a red far more dazzling than that from the walls, with which no brush of antiquity, but young nature of the present, had painted the ground. The former artistic pavement lay

completely ruined, fallen to decay and weather worn; it was
May which exercised here again its most ancient dominion
and covered the whole *oecus*, as it did at the time in many
houses of the buried city, with red, flowering wild poppies,
whose seeds the winds had carried thither, and these had
sprouted in the ashes. It was a wave of densely crowded
blossoms, or so it appeared, although in reality they stood
there motionless, for Atabulus found no way down to them,
but only hummed away softly above. Yet the sun cast such
flaming, radiant vibrations down upon them that it gave
an impression of red ripples in a pond undulating hither and
thither. Norbert Hanold's eyes had passed unheeding over
a similar sight in other houses, but here he was strangely
thrilled by it. The dream-flower grown at the edge of Lethe
filled the space, and Hypnos lay stretched in their midst
dispensing sleep, which dulls the senses, with the saps which
night has gathered in the red chalices. It seemed to the man
who had entered the dining room through the portico of
the peristyle as if he felt his temples touched by the invisible
slumber wand of the old vanquisher of gods and men, but
not with heavy stupor; only a dreamily sweet loveliness
floated about his consciousness. At the same time, however,
he still remained in control of his feet and stepped along by
the wall of the former dining room from which gazed old
pictures: Paris awarding the apple; a satyr carrying in his
hand an asp and tormenting a young Bacchante with it.

But there again suddenly, unforeseen—only about five
paces away from him—in the narrow shadow cast down by
a single piece of the upper part of the dining-room portico,
which still remained in a state of preservation, sitting on the
low steps between two of the yellow pillars was a brightly

clad woman, who now raised her head. In that way she disclosed to the unnoticed arrival, whose footstep she had apparently just heard, a full view of her face, which produced in him a double feeling, for it appeared to him at the same time unknown and yet also familiar, already seen or imagined. But by his arrested breathing and his heart palpitations, he recognized, unmistakably, to whom it belonged. He had found what he was looking for, what had driven him unconsciously to Pompeii; Gradiva continued her visible existence in the noonday spirit hour and sat here before him, as, in the dream, he had seen her on the steps of the Temple of Apollo. Spread out on her knees lay something white which he was unable to distinguish clearly; it seemed to be a papyrus sheet, and a red poppy-blossom stood out from it in marked contrast.

In her face surprise was expressed; under the lustrous brown hair and the beautiful alabaster brow, two unusually bright, starlike eyes looked at him with questioning amazement. It required only a few moments for him to recognize the conformity of her features with those of the profile. They must be thus, viewed from the front, and therefore, at first glance, they had not been really unfamiliar to him. Close to, her white dress, by its slight tendency to yellow, heightened still more the warm color; apparently it consisted of a fine, extremely soft woolen material, which produced abundant folds, and the scarf around her head was of the same. Below, on the nape of the neck, appeared again the shimmering brown hair, artlessly gathered in a single knot; at her throat, under a dainty chin, a little gold clasp, held her gown together.

Norbert Hanold dimly perceived that involuntarily he had

raised his hand to his soft Panama hat and removed it; and now he said in Greek, "Are you Atalanta, the daughter of Jason, or are you a descendant of the family of the poet, Meleager?"

Without giving an answer, the lady he had addressed looked at him silently with a calmly wise expression in her eyes and two thoughts passed through his mind: either her resurrected self could not speak, or she was not of Greek descent and was ignorant of the language. He therefore substituted Latin for it and asked: "Was your father a distinguished Pompeiian citizen of Latin origin?"

To this she was equally silent, except that about her delicately curved lips there was a slight quiver as if she were repressing a burst of laughter. Now a feeling of fright came upon him; apparently she was sitting there before him like a silent image, a phantom to whom speech was denied. Consternation at this discovery was stamped fully and distinctly upon his features.

Then, however, her lips could no longer resist the impulse; a real smile played about them and at the same time a voice sounded from between them: "If you wish to speak with me, you must do so in German."

That was really remarkable from the mouth of a Pompeiian woman who had died two millennia before, or would have been so for a person hearing it in a different state of mind. Yet every oddity escaped Norbert because of two waves of emotion which had rushed over him—one because Gradiva possessed the power of speech, and the other one forced from his inmost being by her voice. It sounded as clear as her glance. Not sharp, but reminiscent of the tones of a bell, her voice passed through the sunny silence over the bloom-

ing poppy-field, and the young archaeologist suddenly realized that he had already heard it thus in his imagination.
Involuntarily he gave audible expression to his feeling: "I
knew that your voice would sound like that."

One could read in her countenance that she was seeking
comprehension of something, but was not finding it. To his
last remark she now responded, "How could you? You have
never talked with me."

To him it was not at all remarkable that she spoke German, and, according to present usage, addressed him for-
mally; as she did it, he understood completely that it could
not have happened otherwise and he answered quickly,
"No—not talked—but I called to you when you lay down to
sleep and stood near you then—your face was as calmly
beautiful as if it were of marble. May I beg you—rest it
again on the step in that way."

While he was speaking, something peculiar had occurred.
A golden butterfly, faintly tinged with red on the inner edge
of its upper wing, fluttered from the poppies toward the
pillars, flitted a few times about Gradiva's head, and then
rested on the brown wavy hair above her brow. At the same
time, however, she rose, slender and tall, for she stood up
with deliberate haste, curtly and silently directed at Norbert
another glance, in which something suggested that she considered him demented. Then, thrusting her foot forward,
she walked out in her characteristic way along the pillars of
the old portico. Only fleetingly visible for a while, she finally
seemed to have sunk into the earth.

He stood up, breathless, as if stunned; yet with heavy
understanding, he had grasped what had occurred before
his eyes. The noonday ghost hour was over and, in the form

of a butterfly, a wingèd messenger had come up from the asphodel meadows of Hades to admonish the departed one to return. For him something else was associated with this, although in confused indistinctness. He knew that the beautiful butterfly of Mediterranean countries bore the name Cleopatra, and this had also been the name of Caledonian Meleager's young wife who, in grief over his death, had given herself as sacrifice to those of the under world.

From his mouth issued a call to the girl who was departing: "Are you coming here again tomorrow in the noon hour?" Yet she did not turn around, gave no answer, and disappeared after a few moments in the corner of the dining room behind the pillar. Now a compelling impulse suddenly incited him to hasten after her, but her bright dress was no longer visible anywhere. Glowing with the hot sun's rays, the Casa di Meleagro lay about him motionless and silent; only Cleopatra hovered on her red, shimmering, golden wings, making slow circles again above the multitude of poppies.

When and how he had returned to the *ingresso*, Norbert Hanold could not recall; in his memory he retained only the idea that his appetite had peremptorily demanded to be appeased, though very tardily, at the Diomede. And then he had wandered forth aimlessly on the first good street, had arrived at the beach north of Castellamare, where he had seated himself on a lava-block, and the sea-wind had blown around his head until the sun had set about halfway between Monte Sant' Angelo above Sorrento and Monte Epomeo on Ischia. Yet, in spite of this stay of at least several hours by the water, he had obtained from the fresh air there no mental relief, but was returning to the hotel in the same condition in which he had left it.

He found the other guests busily occupied with dinner, had a little bottle of Vesuvio wine brought to him in a corner of the room, viewed the faces of those eating, and listened to their conversations. From the faces of all, as well as from their talk, it appeared to him absolutely certain that in the noon hour none of them had either met or spoken to a dead Pompeiian woman who had returned again briefly to life. Of course all this had been a foregone conclusion, as they had all been at lunch at that time. Why and wherefore he himself could not state; yet after a while he went over to the competitor of the Diomed, the Hotel Suisse, sat down there also in a corner, and, as he had to order something, likewise before a little bottle of Vesuvio; and here he gave himself over to the same kind of investigations with eye and ear. They led to the same results but also to the further conclusion that he now knew by sight all the temporary, living visitors of Pompeii. To be sure, this effected an increase of his knowledge which he could hardly consider an enrichment; but from it he experienced a certain satisfying feeling that, in the two hostelries, no guest, either male or female, was present with whom, by means of sight and hearing, he had not entered into a personal, even if one-sided, relation. Of course, in no way had the absurd supposition entered his mind that he might possibly meet Gradiva in one of the two hotels, but he could have taken his oath that no one was staying in them who possessed, in the remotest way, any trace of resemblance to her.

During his observations, he had occasionally poured wine

from his little bottle to his glass, and had drunk from time to time; and when, in this manner, the former had gradually become empty, he rose and went back to the Diomede. The heavens were now strewn with countless, flashing, twinkling stars, but not in the traditionally stationary way, for Norbert gathered the impression that Perseus, Cassiopeia, and Andromeda with some neighbors, bowing lightly hither and thither, were performing a singing dance, and below, on earth, too, it seemed to him that the dark shadows of the treetops and buildings did not stay in the same place. Of course on the ground of this region—unsteady from ancient times—this could not be exactly surprising, for the subterranean glow lurked everywhere, after an eruption, and let a little of itself rise in the vines and grapes from which was pressed Vesuvio, which was not one of Norbert Hanold's usual evening drinks. He still remembered, however, even if a little of the circular movement of things might be ascribed to the wine, too, that since noon all objects had displayed an inclination to whirl softly about his head, and therefore he found, in the slight increase, nothing new, but only a continuation of the formerly existing conditions.

He went up to his room and stood for a little while at the open window, looking over toward the Vesuvius mound, above which now no cone of smoke spread over its top, but rather something like the fluctuations of a dark, purple cloak flowed back and forth around it. Then the young archaeologist undressed, without having lighted the light, and sought his couch. Yet, as he stretched himself out upon it, it was not his bed at the Diomede, but a red poppy-field whose blossoms closed over him like a soft cushion heated by the sun. His enemy, the common housefly, constrained by darkness to lethargic stupidity, sat fiftyfold above his head, on the wall, and only one, moved, even in its sleepiness, by desire to torture, buzzed about his nose. He recognized it, however, not as the absolute evil, the century-old scourge of humanity, for before his eyes it poised like a red-gold Cleopatra.

When in the morning the sun, with lively assistance from the flies, awoke him, he could not recall what, besides strange, Ovid-like metamorphoses, had occurred during the night about his bed. Yet doubtless some mystic being, continuously weaving dream-webs, had been sitting beside him, for he felt his head completely overhung and filled with them, so that all ability to think lay inextricably imprisoned in it and only one thing remained in his consciousness: he must again be in the house of Meleager at exactly noon. In this connection, however, a fear overcame him, for if the gatekeepers at the *ingresso* looked at him they would not let him in. Anyway it was not advisable that he should expose himself to close observation by human eyes. To escape this there was, for one well informed about Pompeii, a means which was, to be sure, against the rules; but he was not in a condition to grant to legal regulation a determination of his conduct. So he climbed again, as on the evening of his arrival, along the old city wall, and upon it walked, in a wide semicircle, around the city of ruins to the solitary, unguarded Porta di Nola. Here it was not difficult to get down into the inside and he went, without burdening his conscience very much over the fact that by his autocratic deed he had deprived the administration of a two-lira entrance fee, which he could, of course, let it have later in some other way.

Thus, unseen, he had reached an uninteresting part of the city, never before investigated by any one and still mostly unexcavated; he sat down in a secluded, shady nook and waited, now and then drawing out his watch to observe the progress of time. Once his glance fell upon something in the distance, gleaming silvery-white, rising from the ashes; but with his unreliable vision he was unable to distinguish what it was. Yet involuntarily he was impelled to go up to it and there it stood, a tall, flowering asphodel plant with white, bell-like blossoms whose seeds the wind had carried thither from outside. It was the flower of the underworld, significant and, as he felt, destined to grow here for his purpose. He broke the slender stem and returned with it to his seat. Hotter and hotter the May sun burned down as on the day before, and finally approached its noonday position; so now he started out through the long Strada di Nola. This lay deathly still and deserted, as did almost all the others; over there to the west all the morning visitors were already crowding again to the Porta Marina and the soup-plates. Only the air, suffused with heat, stirred, and in the dazzling glare the solitary figure of Norbert Hanold with the asphodel branch appeared like that of Hermes, Psyche's escort, in modern attire, starting out upon the journey to conduct a departed soul to Hades.

Not consciously, yet following an instinctive impulse, he found his way through the Strada della Fortuna farther along to the Strada di Mercurio, and turning to the right he arrived at the Casa di Meleagro. Just as lifelessly as yesterday, the vestibule, inner court, and peristyle received him, and between the pillars of the latter the poppies of the dining room flamed across to him. As he entered, however, it was not clear to him whether he had been here yesterday or two thousand years ago to seek from the owner of the house some information of great importance to archaeology; what it was, however, he could not state, and besides, it seemed to him, even though in contradiction to the above, that all the science of antiquity was the most purposeless and indifferent thing in the world. He could not understand how a human being could occupy himself with it, for there was only a single thing to which all thinking and investigation must be directed: what was the nature of the physical manifestation of a being like Gradiva, dead and alive at the same time, although the latter was true only in the noon hour of spirits—or had been the day before, perhaps the one time in a century or a thousand years, for it suddenly seemed certain that his return today was in vain. He would not meet the girl he was looking for, because she was not allowed to come again until a time when he too would have been dead for many years, and would be buried and forgotten.

Of course, as he walked now along by the wall below Paris awarding the apple, he perceived Gradiva before him, just as on yesterday, in the same gown, sitting between the same two yellow pillars on the same step. Yet he did not allow himself to be deceived by tricks of imagination, but knew that fancy alone was deceptively depicting before his eyes what he had really seen there the day before. He could not refrain, however, from stopping to indulge in the view of the shadowy apparition created by himself and, without his knowing it, there passed from his lips in a grieved tone the words, "Oh, that you were still alive!"

His voice rang out, but then breathless silence again reigned among the ruins of the old dining room. Yet soon another sounded through the vacant stillness, saying, "Won't you sit down too? You look exhausted."

Norbert Hanold's heart stood still a moment. His head, however, collected this much reason: a vision could not speak; or was an aural hallucination practicing deception upon him? With fixed gaze, he supported himself against the pillar.

Then again asked the voice, and it was the one which none other than Gradiva possessed, "Are you bringing me the white flowers?"

Dizziness rushed upon him; he felt that his feet no longer supported him, but forced him to be seated; and he slid down opposite her on the step, against the pillar. Her bright eyes were directed toward his face, yet with a different look from the one with which she had gazed at him yesterday when she suddenly rose and went away. In that, something ill-humored and aloof had spoken; but it had disappeared, as if she had, in the meanwhile, arrived at a different viewpoint, and an expression of searching curiosity and inquisitiveness had taken its place. Likewise, she spoke with an easy familiarity. As he remained silent, however, to the last question also, she again resumed: "You told me yesterday that you had once called to me when I lay down to sleep and that you had afterwards stood near me; my face was as white as marble. When and where was that? I cannot remember it and I beg you to explain more exactly."

Norbert had now acquired enough power of speech to answer, "In the night when you sat on the steps of the Temple of Apollo in the Forum and the fall of ashes from Vesuvius covered you."

"So—then. Yes, to be sure—that had not occurred to me,

but I might have thought that it would be a case like that. When you said it yesterday, I was not expecting it and I was utterly unprepared. Yet that happened, if I recall correctly, two thousand years ago. Were you living then? It seems to me you look younger."

She spoke very seriously, but at the end a faint, extremely sweet smile played about her mouth. He hesitated in embarrassment and answered, stuttering slightly, "No, I really don't believe I was alive in the year 79—it was perhaps— yes, it surely is a psychic condition which is called a dream that transported me into the time of the destruction of Pompeii—but I recognized you again at first glance."

In the expression of the girl sitting opposite him, a few feet away, surprise was apparent and she repeated in a tone of amazement, "You recognized me again? In the dream? By what?"

"At the very first; by your manner of walking."

"Had you noticed that? And have I a special manner of walking?"

Her astonishment had grown perceptibly. He replied, "Yes—don't you realize that? A more graceful one—at least among those now living—does not exist. Yet I recognized you immediately by everything else too, your figure, face, bearing and drapery, for everything agreed most minutely with the bas-relief of you in Rome."

"Ah, really," she repeated in her former tone, "with the bas-relief of me in Rome. Yes, I hadn't thought of that either, and at this moment I don't know exactly—what is it—and you saw it there then?"

Now he told her that the sight of it had attracted him so that he had been highly pleased to get a plaster cast of it in Germany and that for years it had hung in his room. He observed it daily and the idea had come to him that it must represent a young Pompeiian girl who was walking on the steppingstones of a street in her native city; and the dream had confirmed it. Now he knew also that he had been impelled by it to travel here again to see whether he could find some trace of her; and as he had stood yesterday noon at the corner of the Strada di Mercurio, she herself, exactly like her image, had suddenly walked before him across the steppingstones, as if she were about to go over into the house of Apollo. Then farther along she had recrossed the street and disappeared before the house of Meleager.

To this she nodded and said, "Yes, I intended to look up the house of Apollo, but I came here."

He continued, "On that account the Greek poet, Meleager, came to my mind and I thought that you were one of his descendants and were returning—in the hour which you are allowed—to your ancestral home. When I spoke to you in Greek, however, you did not understand."

"Was that Greek? No, I don't understand it, or I've probably forgotten it. Yet as you came again just now, I heard you say something that I could understand. You expressed the wish that someone might still be alive here. Only I did not understand whom you meant by that."

That caused him to reply that, at sight of her, he had believed that it was not really she, but that his imagination was deceptively putting her image before him in the place where he had met her yesterday. At that she smiled and agreed: "It seems that you have reason to be on your guard against an excess of imagination, although, when I have been with you, I never supposed so." She stopped, however,

and added, "What is there peculiar about my way of walking, which you spoke of before?"

It was noteworthy that her aroused interest brought her
back to that, and he said, "If I may ask—"

With that he stopped, for he suddenly remembered with
fear that yesterday she had suddenly risen and gone away
when he had asked her to lie down to sleep again on that
step, as on that of the Temple of Apollo; and, associated
darkly with this, there came to him the glance which she
had directed upon him in departing. Yet now the calm,
friendly expression of her eyes remained. And, as he spoke
no further, she said, "It was nice that your wish that someone might still be alive concerned me. If you wish to ask
anything of me on that account, I will gladly respond."

That overcame his fear, and he replied, "It would make
me happy to get a close view of you walking as you do in
the bas-relief."

Willingly, without answering, she stood up and walked
along between the wall and the pillars. It was the very
buoyantly reposeful gait, with the sole raised almost perpendicularly, that was so firmly imprinted on his mind; but for
the first time he saw that she wore, below the raised gown,
not sandals, but light, sand-colored shoes of fine leather.
When she came back and sat down again silently, he involuntarily started to talk of the difference in her footgear
from that of the bas-relief. To that she rejoined, "Time, of
course, always changes everything, and for the present sandals are not suitable, so I put on shoes, which are a better
protection against rain and dust; but why did you ask me
to walk before you? What is there peculiar about it?"

Her repeated wish to learn this proved her not entirely

free from feminine curiosity. He now explained that it was a matter of the peculiarly upright position of the rising foot, as she walked, and he added how for weeks he had tried to observe the gait of modern women on the streets in his native city. Yet it seemed that this beautiful way of walking had been completely lost to them, with the exception, perhaps, of a single one who had given him the impression that she walked in that way. To be sure, he had not been able to establish this fact because of the crowd about her, and he had probably experienced an illusion, for it had seemed to him that her features had resembled somewhat those of Gradiva.

"What a shame," she answered. "For confirmation of the fact would surely have been of great scientific importance, and if you had succeeded, perhaps you would not have needed to take the long journey here. But whom were you just speaking of? Who is Gradiva?"

"I have named the bas-relief that, because I didn't know your real name and don't know it yet, either."

This last he added with some hesitancy, and she faltered a moment before replying to the indirect question, "My name is Zoë."

With pained tone the words escaped him: "The name suits you beautifully, but it sounds to me like bitter mockery, for 'Zoë' means 'life.'"

"One must resign oneself to the inevitable," she responded. "And I have long accustomed myself to being dead. But now my time is over for today; you have brought the grave-flower with you to conduct me back. So give it to me."

As she rose and stretched forth her slender hand, he gave her the asphodel cluster but was careful not to touch her fingers. Accepting the flowering branch, she said, "I thank you. To those who are more fortunate one gives roses in spring, but for me the flower of oblivion is the right one from your hand. Tomorrow I shall be allowed to come here again at this hour. If your way leads you again into the house of Meleager, we can sit together at the edge of the poppies, as we did today. On the threshold is written, 'Ave,' and I say it to you, 'Ave'!"

She went out and disappeared, as yesterday, at the turn in the portico, as if she had there sunk into the ground. Everything lay empty and silent again, but from a distance there once rang, short and clear, a sound like the merry note of a bird flying over the devastated city. This was stifled immediately, however. Norbert, who had remained behind, looked down at the step where she had just been sitting. There something white shimmered; it seemed to be the papyrus leaf which Gradiva had held on her knees yesterday and had forgotten to take with her today. Yet as he shyly reached for it, he found it to be a little sketchbook with pencil drawings of the different ruins in several houses of Pompeii. The page next to the last showed a drawing of the griffin-table in the central court of the Casa di Meleagro, and on the last was the beginning of a reproduction of the view across the poppies of the dining room through the row of pillars of the peristyle. That the departed girl made drawings in a sketchbook of the present mode was as amazing as had been the fact that she expressed her thoughts in German. Yet those were only insignificant prodigies beside the great one of her revivification, and apparently she used the midday hour of freedom to preserve for herself, in their present state, with unusual artistic talent, the surroundings in which she had once lived. The drawings testified to delicately cultivated powers of perception, as each of her words did to a clever intellect; and she had probably often sat by the old griffin-table, so that it was a particularly precious reminder. Mechanically Norbert also went, with the little book, along the portico; and, at the place where this turned, he noticed in the wall a narrow cleft wide enough to afford, to an unusually slender figure, passage into the adjoining building, and even farther to the Vicolo del Fauno at the other side of the house. Suddenly, however, the idea flashed through his mind that Zoë-Gradiva did not sink into the ground here —that was essentially unreasonable, and he could not understand how he had ever believed it—but went, on this route, back to her tomb. That must be in the Street of Tombs. Rushing forth, he hastened out into the Strada di Mercurio and as far as the gate of Hercules; but when, breathless and reeking with perspiration, he entered this, it was already too late. The broad Strada di Sepolcri stretched out empty and dazzlingly white; only at its extremity, behind the glimmering curtain of radiance, a faint shadow seemed to dissolve uncertainly before the Villa of Diomede.

Norbert Hanold passed the second half of the day with a feeling that Pompeii was everywhere, or at least wherever he stopped, veiled in a cloud of mist. It was not grey, gloomy, and melancholy as formerly, but rather cheerful and vari-colored to an extraordinary degree, blue, red and brown, chiefly a light-yellowish white and alabaster white, inter-woven with golden threads of sunbeams. This injured neither his power of vision nor that of hearing; but, because of it, thinking was impossible, and that produced a cloud-wall

whose effect rivaled the thickest mist. To the young archaeologist it seemed almost as if hourly, in an invisible and not
otherwise noticeable way, there was brought to him a little
bottle of Vesuvio wine, which produced a continuous whirling in his head. From this he instinctively sought to free
himself by the use of correctives, on the one hand drinking
water frequently, and on the other hand moving about as
much and as far as possible. His knowledge of medicine was
not comprehensive, but it helped him to the diagnosis that
this strange condition must arise from excessive congestion
of blood in his head, perhaps associated with accelerated
action of the heart; for he felt the latter—something formerly quite unknown to him—occasionally beating fast
against his chest. Otherwise, his thoughts, which could not
penetrate into the outer world, were not in the least inactive
within—or, more exactly, there was only one thought there,
which had come into sole possession and carried on a restless
though vain activity. It continually turned about the question of what physical nature Zoë-Gradiva might possess,
whether during her stay in the house of Meleager she was
a corporeal being or only an illusory representation of what
she had formerly been. For the former, physical, physiological, and anatomical facts seemed to argue that she had at
her disposal organs of speech and could hold a pencil with
her fingers. Yet Norbert was overwhelmed with the idea
that if he should touch her, even lightly place his hand on
hers, he would then encounter only empty air. A peculiar
impulse urged him to make sure of this, but an equally
great timidity hindered him from even thinking of doing it.
For he felt that the confirmation of either of the two possibilities must bring with it something inspiring fear. The

corporeal existence of the hand would thrill him with horror, and its lack of substance would cause him deep pain.

Occupied vainly with this problem, which was impossible to solve scientifically without experiment, he arrived, in the course of his extensive wanderings that afternoon, at the foothills of the big mountain group of Monte Sant' Angelo, rising south from Pompeii, and here he unexpectedly came upon an elderly man, already gray-bearded, who, from his equipment with all sorts of implements, seemed to be a zoologist or botanist and appeared to be making a search on a hot, sunny slope. He turned his head, as Norbert came close to him, looked at the latter in surprise for a moment and then said, "Are you interested in *Faraglionensis*, too? I should hardly have supposed it, but to me it seems not at all unlikely that it not only dwells in the *Faraglioni* of Capri, but also can with some perseverance be found on the mainland. The method suggested by my colleague, Eimer, is really good; I have already used it often with the best of success. Please keep quite still—"

The speaker stopped, stepped carefully forward a few paces and, stretched out motionless on the ground, held a little snare, made of a long blade of grass, before a narrow crevice in the rock, from which the blue, chatoyant little head of a lizard peeped. Thus the man remained without the slightest movement, and Norbert Hanold turned about noiselessly behind him and returned by the way he had come. It seemed to him dimly that he had already seen the face of the lizard-hunter, probably in one of the two hotels; to this fact the latter's manner pointed. It was hardly credible what odd and crazy projects could cause people to make the long trip to Pompeii; happy that he had suc-

ceeded in so quickly ridding himself of the snare-layer, and
being again able to direct his thoughts to the problem of
corporeal reality or unreality, he started on the return.

Yet a side street misled him once to a wrong turn and took
him, instead of to the west boundary, to the east end of the
extensive old city wall; buried in thought, he did not notice
the mistake until he had come right up to a building which
was neither the Diomede nor the Hotel Suisse. In spite of this
it bore the sign of a hotel; nearby he recognized the ruins
of the large Pompeiian amphitheater, and the memory came
to him that, near this latter, there was another hotel, the
"Albergo del Sole," which, on account of its remoteness
from the station, was sought out by only a few guests and
had remained unknown to even him. The walk had made
him hot; besides, the cloudy whirling in his head had not
diminished; so he stepped in through the open door and
ordered the remedy deemed useful by him for blood congestion, a bottle of limewater. The room stood empty except, of course, for the fly-visitors gathered in full numbers,
and the unoccupied host availed himself of the opportunity
to recommend highly his house and the excavated treasures
it contained. He pointed suggestively to the fact that there
were, near Pompeii, people at whose places there was not
a single genuine piece among the many objects offered for
sale, but that all were imitations; whereas he, satisfying
himself with a smaller number, offered his guests only
things undoubtedly genuine. For he acquired no articles
which he himself had not seen brought to the light of day;
and, in the course of his eloquence, he revealed that he had
also been present when they had found near the Forum the

young lovers who had clasped each other in firm embrace when they realized their inevitable destruction and had thus awaited death. Norbert had already heard of this discovery, but had shrugged his shoulders about it as a fabulous invention of some especially imaginative narrator; and he did so now, too, when the host brought in to him, as authentic proof, a metal brooch encrusted with green patina, which, in his presence, had been gathered from the ashes along with the remains of the girl. When the arrival at the Sun Hotel took it in his own hand, however, the power of imagination exercised such ascendency over him that suddenly, without further critical consideration, he paid for it the price asked from English people, and, with his acquisition, hastily left the "Albergo del Sole," in which, after another turn, he saw, in an open window, nodding down, an asphodel branch covered with white blossoms, which had been placed in a water glass; and, without needing any logical connection, it rushed through his mind, at the sight of the grave-flower, that it was an attestation of the genuineness of his new possession.

This he viewed with mingled feelings of excitement and shyness, keeping now to the way along the city wall to Porta Marina. Then it was no fairy tale that a couple of young lovers had been excavated near the Forum in such an embrace, and there at the Temple of Apollo he had seen Gradiva lie down to sleep, but only in a dream; that he knew now quite definitely; in reality she might have gone on still farther from the Forum, met someone, and died with him.

From the green brooch between his fingers a feeling passed through him that it had belonged to Zoë-Gradiva, and had held her dress closed at the throat. Then she was the beloved fiancée, perhaps the young wife, of the man with whom she had wished to die.

It occurred to Norbert Hanold to hurl the brooch away. It burned his fingers as if it had become glowing, or, more exactly, it caused him the pain such as he had felt at the idea that he might put his hand on that of Gradiva and encounter only empty air.

Reason, nevertheless, asserted the upper hand; he did not allow himself to be controlled by imagination against his will. However probable it might be, there was still lacking invincible proof that the brooch had belonged to her and that it had been she who had been discovered in the young man's arms. This judgment made it possible for him to breathe freely, and when, at the dawn of twilight, he reached the Diomede, his long wandering had brought to his sound constitution need of physical refreshment.

Not without appetite did he devour the rather Spartan evening meal which the Diomede, in spite of its Argive origin, had adopted; and he then noticed two guests, newly arrived in the course of the afternoon. By appearance and language they marked themselves as Germans, a man and a woman; they both had youthful, attractive features endowed with intellectual expressions. Their relation to each other could not be determined; yet, because of a certain resemblance, Norbert decided that they were brother and sister. To be sure the young man's fair hair differed in color from her light-brown tresses. On her gown she wore a red Sorrento rose, the sight of which, as he looked across from the corner, stirred something in his memory without his being able to think what it was. The couple were the first people he had met on his journey who seemed possibly congenial. They talked with one another, over a little bottle, in not too plainly audible tones, nor in cautious whisperings, apparently sometimes about serious things and sometimes about gay things, for at times there passed over her face a half-laughing expression which was very becoming to her, and aroused the desire to participate in their conversation, or perhaps might have awakened it in Norbert, if he had met them two days before in the room otherwise populated only by Anglo-Americans. Yet he felt that what was passing through his mind stood in too strong contrast to the happy naïveté of the couple about whom there undeniably lay not the slightest cloud, for they doubtless were not meditating profoundly over the essential nature of a girl who had died two thousand years ago, but, without any weariness, were taking pleasure in an enigmatical problem of their life of the present. His condition did not harmonize with that; on the one hand he seemed superfluous to them, and on the other he recoiled from an attempt to start an acquaintance with them, for he had a dark feeling that their bright, merry eyes might look through his forehead into his thoughts and thereby assume an expression as if they did not consider him quite in his right mind.

Therefore he went up to his room, stood as yesterday at the window, looking over to the purple night-mantle of Vesuvius, and then lay down to rest. Exhausted, he soon fell asleep and dreamed, but remarkably nonsensically. Somewhere in the sun Gradiva sat making a trap out of a blade of grass, in order to catch a lizard, and she said: "Please stay quite still—my colleague is right; the method is really good, and she has used it with the greatest success!"

Norbert Hanold became conscious in his dream that it was actually the most utter madness, and he cast about to free himself from it. He succeeded in this by the aid of an invisible bird, who seemingly uttered a short, merry call, and carried the lizard away in its beak; afterwards everything disappeared.

On awakening, he remembered that in the night a voice had said that in the spring one gave roses; or rather this was recalled to him through his eyes, for his gaze, passing down from the window, came upon a bright bush of red flowers. They were of the same kind as those which the young lady had worn in her bosom, and when he went down he involuntarily plucked a couple and smelled them. In fact, there must be something peculiar about Sorrento roses, for their fragrance seemed to him not only wonderful but quite new and unfamiliar, and at the same time he felt that they had a somewhat liberating effect upon his mind.

At least they freed him from yesterday's timidity before the gatekeepers, for he went, according to directions, in through the *ingresso* to Pompeii, paid double the amount of admission fee, and quickly struck out upon streets which took him from the vicinity of other visitors. The little sketch-book, from the house of Meleager, he carried along with the green brooch and the red roses, but the fragrance of the latter had made him forget to eat breakfast and his thoughts were not in the present, but were directed exclusively to the noon hour which was still far off. He had to pass the remaining interval, and for this purpose he entered now one house, now another, as a result of which activity the idea probably occurred to him that Gradiva had also walked there often before or even now sought these places out sometimes—his supposition that she was able to do it only at noon was tottering. Perhaps she was at liberty to do it in other hours of the day, possibly even at night in the moonlight.

The roses strengthened this supposition strangely for him, when he inhaled as he held them to his nose. And his deliberations, complaisant, and open to conviction, made advances to this new idea, for he could bear witness that he did not cling to preconceived opinions at all, but rather gave free rein to every reasonable objection, and such there was here, without any doubt, not only logically but desirably valid. Only the question arose whether, upon meeting her then, the eyes of others could see her as a corporeal being, or whether only his possessed the ability to do that. The former was not to be denied, claimed even probability for itself, transformed the desirable thing into quite the opposite, and transported him into a low-spirited, restless mood. The thought that others might also speak to her, and sit down near her to carry on a conversation with her, made him indignant. To that he alone possessed a claim, or at any rate a privilege; for he had discovered Gradiva, of whom no one had formerly known, had observed her daily, taken her into his life, to a degree, imparted to her his life-strength, and it seemed to him as if he had thereby again lent to her life that she would not have possessed without him. Therefore he felt that there devolved upon him a right to which he alone might make a claim and which he might refuse to share with anyone else.

The advancing day was hotter than the two preceding; the sun seemed to have set her mind today on a quite ex-

traordinary feat, and made it regrettable, not only in an
archaeological but also in a practical connection, that the
water system of Pompeii had lain burst and dried up for
two thousand years. Street fountains here and there com-
memorated it and likewise gave evidence of their informal
use by thirsty passers-by, who had, in order to bend forward
to the jet, leaned a hand on the marble railing and gradually
dug out a sort of trough in the place, in the same way that
dripping wears away stone. Norbert observed this at a
corner of the Strada della Fortuna, and from that the idea
occurred to him that the hand of Zoë-Gradiva, too, might
formerly have rested here in that way, and involuntarily he
laid his hand into the little hollow; yet he immediately rejected the idea, and felt annoyance at himself that he could
have done it. The thought did not harmonize at all with the
nature and bearing of the young Pompeiian girl of a refined
family; there was something profane in the idea that she
could have bent over so and placed her lips on the very pipe
from which the plebeians drank with coarse mouths. In a
noble sense, he had never seen anything more seemly than
her actions and movements. He was frightened by the idea
that she might be able to see by looking at him that he had
had the incredibly unreasonable thought, for her eyes possessed something penetrating; a couple of times, when he
had been with her, the feeling had seized him that she
looked as if she were seeking for access to his inmost
thoughts and were looking about them as if with a bright
steel probe. He was obliged, therefore, to take great care
that she might come upon nothing foolish in his mental
processes.

It was now an hour until noon, and in order to pass the

time, he went diagonally across the street into the Casa del Fauno, the most extensive and magnificent of all the excavated houses. Like no other, it possessed a double inner court and showed, in the larger one, on the middle of the ground, the empty base on which had stood the famous statue of the dancing faun after which the house had been named. Yet there stirred in Norbert Hanold not the least regret that this work of art, valued highly by science, was no longer here, but, together with the mosaic picture of the Battle of Alexander, had been transferred to the Museo Nazionale in Naples; he possessed no further intention nor desire than to let time move along, and he wandered about aimlessly in this place through the large building. Behind the peristyle opened a wider room, surrounded by numerous pillars, planned either as another repetition of the peristyle or as an ornamental garden; so it seemed at present for, like the dining room of the Casa di Meleagro, it was completely covered with poppy blooms. Absent-mindedly the visitor passed through the silent dereliction.

Then, however, he stopped and rested on one foot. But he found himself not alone here; at some distance his glance fell upon two figures, who first gave the impression of only one, because they stood as closely as possible to each other. They did not see him, for they were concerned only with themselves, and, in that corner, because of the pillars, might have believed themselves undiscoverable by any other eyes. Embracing each other, they held their lips also pressed together and the unsuspected spectator recognized, to his amazement, that they were the young man and woman who had last evening seemed to him the first congenial people encountered on this trip. For brother and sister, their present position, the embrace and the kiss, it seemed to him, had lasted too long. So it was surely another pair of lovers, probably a young bridal couple, an Augustus and Gretchen, too.

Strange to relate, however, the two latter did not, at the moment, enter Norbert's mind, and the incident seemed to him not at all ridiculous nor repulsive; rather it heightened his pleasure in them. What they were doing seemed to him as natural as it did comprehensible; his eyes clung to the living picture, more widely open than they ever had been to any of the most admired works of art, and he would have gladly devoted himself for a longer time to his observation. Yet it seemed to him that he had wrongfully penetrated into a consecrated place and was on the point of disturbing a secret act of devotion; the idea of being noticed there struck terror to his heart and he quickly turned, went back some distance noiselessly on tiptoe and, when he had passed beyond hearing distance, ran out with bated breath and beating heart to the Vicolo del Fauno.

When he arrived before the house of Meleager, he did not know whether it was already noon and did not happen to question his watch about it, but remained before the door, standing looking down with indecision for some time at the "Ave" in the entrance. A fear prevented him from stepping in. Strangely, he was equally afraid of not meeting Gradiva within, and of finding her there; for, during the last few moments, he had felt quite sure that, in the first case, she would be staying somewhere else with some younger man, and, in the second case, the latter would be in company with her on the steps between the pillars. Toward the man, however, he felt a hate far stronger than against all the assembled common houseflies; until today he had not considered it possible that he could be capable of such violent inner excitement. The duel, which he had always considered stupid nonsense, suddenly appeared to him in a different light; here it became a natural right which the man injured in his own rights, or mortally insulted, made use of as the only available means to secure satisfaction or to part with an existence which had become purposeless. So he suddenly stepped forward to enter; he would challenge the bold man and would—this rushed in upon him almost more powerfully —express unreservedly to her that he had considered her something better, more noble, and incapable of such vulgarity.

He was so filled to the brim with this rebellious idea that he uttered it, even though there was not apparently the least occasion for it. For, when he had covered the distance to the dining room with stormy haste, he demanded violently, "Are you alone?"—although appearances allowed of no doubt that Gradiva was sitting there on the steps, just as much alone as on the two previous days.

She looked at him amazed and replied, "Who should still be here after noon? Then the people are all hungry and sit down to meals. Nature has arranged that very happily for me."

His surging excitement could not, however, be allayed so quickly; and without his knowledge or desire, he let slip, with the conviction of certainty, the conjecture which had come over him outside. For he added, to be sure somewhat foolishly, that he could really not think otherwise.

Her bright eyes remained fixed upon his face until he

had finished. Then she made a motion with one finger against her brow and said, "You—" After that, however, she continued, "It seems to me quite enough that I do not remain away from here, even though I must expect that you are coming here at this time; but the place pleases me and I see that you have brought me my sketchbook which I forgot here yesterday. I thank you for your vigilance. Won't you give it to me?"

The last question was well founded, for he showed no disposition to do so but remained motionless. It began to dawn upon him that he had imagined and worked out a monstrous piece of nonsense, and had also given expression to it; in order to compensate, as far as possible, he now stepped forward hastily, handed Gradiva the book, and at the same time sat down near her on the step, mechanically. Casting a glance at his hand, she said, "You seem to be a lover of roses."

At these words he suddenly became conscious of what had caused him to pluck and bring them and he responded, "Yes—of course, not for myself, have I—you spoke yesterday —and last night, too, someone said it to me—people give them in spring."

She pondered briefly, before she answered, "I see—yes, I remember. To others, I meant, one does not give asphodel, but roses. That is polite of you; it seems your opinion of me is improved."

Her hand stretched out to receive the red flowers, and, handing them to her, he rejoined, "I believed at first that you could be here only during the noon hour, but it has become probable to me that you also, at some other time— that makes me very happy—"

"Why does it make you happy?"

Her face expressed lack of comprehension—only about her lips there passed a slight, hardly noticeable quiver. Confused he offered, "It is beautiful to be alive; it has never seemed so much so to me before—I wished to ask you." He searched in his breast pocket and added, as he drew out the object, "Has this brooch ever belonged to you?"

She leaned forward a little toward it, but shook her head, "No, I can't remember. Chronologically it would, of course, not be impossible, for it probably did not exist until this year. Did you find it in the Sun, perhaps? The beautiful, green patina surely seems familiar to me, as if I had already seen it."

Involuntarily he repeated, "In the sun?—why in the sun?"

" 'Sole' it is called here. It performs such tricks around here. Was the brooch said to have belonged to a young girl who is said to have perished, I believe, in the vicinity of the Forum, with a companion?"

"Yes, who held his arm about her—"

"I see—"

The two little words apparently lay upon Gradiva's tongue as a favorite interjection, and she stopped after it for a moment, before she added, "Did you think that on that account I might have worn it? And would that have made you a little—how did you say it before?—unhappy?"

It was apparent that he felt extraordinarily relieved, and it was audible in his answer, "I am very happy about it—for the idea that the brooch belonged to you made me—dizzy."

"You seem to have a tendency for that. Did you perhaps forget to eat breakfast this morning? That easily aggravates such attacks; I do not suffer from them, but I make provisions, as it suits me best to be here at noon. If I can help you out of your unfortunate condition a little by sharing my lunch with you—"

She drew out of her pocket a piece of white bread wrapped in tissue paper, broke it, put half into his hand, and began to devour the other with apparent appetite. Thereby her exceptionally dainty and perfect teeth not only gleamed between her lips with pearly glitter, but also in biting the crust caused a crunching sound so that they gave the impression of being not unreal phantoms, but of actual, substantial reality. Besides, with her conjecture about the postponed breakfast, she had, to be sure, hit upon the right thing; mechanically he too ate and felt from it a decidedly favorable effect on the clearing of his thoughts. So, for a little while, the couple did not speak further, but devoted themselves silently to the same practical occupation until Gradiva said, "It seems to me as if we had eaten our bread together like this once, two thousand years ago. Can't you remember it?"

He could not, but it seemed strange to him now that she spoke of so infinitely remote a past, for the strengthening of his mind by the nourishment had brought with it a change in his brain. The idea that she had been going around here in Pompeii such a long time ago would no longer harmonize with sound reason; everything about her seemed of the present, as if it could be scarcely more than twenty years old. The form and color of her face, the especially charming, brown wavy hair, and the flawless teeth; also, the idea that the bright dress, marred by no shadow of a spot, had lain countless years in the pumice ashes—this contained something in the highest degree inconsistent. Norbert was seized by a feeling of doubt whether he were really sitting here awake or were not more probably dreaming in his study, where, in contemplation of the likeness of Gradiva, he had been overcome by sleep, and had dreamed that he had gone to Pompeii, had met her as a person still living, and was dreaming further that he was still sitting so at her side in the Casa di Meleagro. For, that she was really still alive or had been living again could only have happened in a dream— the laws of nature raised an objection to it—

To be sure, it was strange that she had just said that she had once shared her bread with him in that way two thousand years ago. Of that he knew nothing and even in the dream could find nothing about it.

Her left hand lay with the slender fingers calmly on her knees. They bore the key to the solution of an inscrutable riddle—

Even in the dining room of the Casa di Meleagro, the boldness of the common housefly was not deterred. On the yellow pillar opposite him he saw one running up and down in a worthless way in greedy quest; now it whizzed right past his nose.

He, however, had to make some answer to her question, if he did not remember the bread that he had formerly consumed with her and he said suddenly, "Were the flies then as devilish as now, so that they tormented you to death?"

She glanced at him with utterly incomprehending astonishment and repeated, "The flies? Have you flies on your mind now?"

Then suddenly the black monster sat upon her hand, which did not reveal by the slightest quiver that she noticed

it. Thereupon, however, there united in the young archaeologist two powerful impulses to execute the same deed. His
hand went up suddenly and clapped with no gentle stroke
on the fly and the hand of his neighbor.

With this blow there came to him, for the first time, sense,
consternation, and also a joyous fear. He had delivered the
stroke not through empty air, but on an undoubtedly real,
living, warm human hand which, for a moment apparently
absolutely startled, remained motionless under his. Yet then
she drew it away with a jerk, and the mouth above it said,
"You are obviously crazy, Norbert Hanold."

The name, which he had disclosed to no one in Pompeii,
passed so easily, assuredly, and clearly from her lips that its
owner jumped up from the steps, even more terrified. At the
same time there sounded in the colonnade footsteps of people who had come near unobserved; before his confused
eyes appeared the faces of the congenial pair of lovers from
the Casa del Fauno, and the young lady cried, with a tone
of greatest surprise, "Zoë! You here, too? And also on your
honeymoon? You haven't written me a word about it, you
know."

Norbert was again outside before the house of Meleager
in the Strada di Mercurio. How he had come there was not
clear to him; it must have happened instinctively, and,
caused by a lightning-like illumination in him, was the only
thing that he could do not to present a thoroughly ridiculous figure to the young couple, even more to the girl
greeted so pleasantly by them, who had just addressed him
by his Christian and family names, and most of all to himself. For, even if he grasped nothing, one fact was indis-

putable. Gradiva, with a warm, human hand, not unsubstan-
tial, but possessing corporeal reality, had expressed an in-
dubitable truth: his mind had, in the last two days, been in
a condition of absolute madness; and not at all in a silly
dream, but rather with the use of eyes and ears such as is
given by nature to man for reasonable service. Like everything else, how such a thing had happened escaped his understanding, and only darkly did he feel that there must
have also been in the game a sixth sense which, obtaining
the upper hand in some way, had transformed something
perhaps precious into the opposite. In order to get at least a
little more light on the matter by an attempt at meditation,
a remote place in solitary silence was absolutely required;
at first, however, he was impelled to withdraw as quickly
as possible from the sphere of eyes, ears, and other senses,
which use their natural functions as suits their own purpose.

As for the owner of that warm hand, she had, at any rate,
from her first expression, been surprised by the unforeseen
and unexpected visit at noon in the Casa di Meleagro in a
not entirely pleasant manner. Yet, of this, in the next instant,
there was no trace to be seen in her bright countenance. She
stood up quickly, stepped toward the young lady and said,
extending her hand, "It certainly is pleasant, Gisa; chance
sometimes has a clever idea too. So this is your husband of
two weeks? I am glad to see him, and, from the appearance
of both of you, I apparently need not change my congratulations for condolence. Couples to whom that would be applied are at this time usually sitting at lunch in Pompeii.
You are probably staying near the *ingresso;* I shall look you
up there this afternoon. No, I have not written you anything; you won't be offended at me for that, for you see my

hand, unlike yours, is not adorned by a ring. The atmosphere here has an extremely powerful effect on the imagination, which I can see in you; it is better, of course, than if it made one too matter-of-fact. The young man who just went away is also laboring under a strange delusion; it seems to me that he believes a fly is buzzing in his head; well, everybody probably has some kind of bee in his bonnet. As is my duty, I have some knowledge of entomology and can, therefore, be of a little service in such cases. My father and I are staying at the 'Sole'; he, too, had a sudden attack and, on top of that, the good idea of bringing me here with him if I agreed to be responsible for my own entertainment and to make no demands upon him. I said to myself that I should certainly dig up something interesting here by myself. Of course I certainly didn't expect the find which I made—I mean the good fortune of meeting you, Gisa; but I am talking away the time, as is usually the case with an old friend— My father comes in out of the sun at two o'clock to eat at the 'Sole'; so I have to keep company there with his appetite and, therefore, I am sorry to say, must, for the moment forgo your society. You will, of course, be able to view the Casa di Meleagro without me; that I think likely, though I can't understand it, of course. *Favorisca, signor! Arrivederci, Gisetta!* That much Italian I have already learned, and one really does not need more. Whatever else is necessary one can invent—please, no, *senza complimenti!*"

This last entreaty of the speaker concerned a polite movement by which the young husband had seemed to wish to escort her. She had expressed herself most vividly, naturally, and in a manner quite fitting to the circumstances of the unexpected meeting of a close friend, yet with extraordinary celerity, which testified to the urgency of the declaration that she could not at present remain longer. So not more than a few minutes had passed since the hasty exit of Norbert Hanold, when she also stepped from the house of Meleager into the Strada di Mercurio. This was, because of the hour, enlivened only here and there by a cringing lizard, and for a few moments the girl, hesitating, apparently gave herself over to a brief meditation. Then she quickly struck out in the shortest way to the gate of Hercules, at the intersection of the Vicolo di Mercurio and the Strada di Sallustio, crossed the steppingstones with the gracefully buoyant Gradiva-walk, and thus arrived very quickly at the two ruins of the side wall near the Porta Ercolanese.

Behind this there stretched at some length the Street of Tombs, yet not dazzlingly white, nor overhung with glittering sunbeams, as twenty-four hours ago, when the young archaeologist had thus gazed down over it with searching eyes. Today the sun seemed to be overcome by a feeling that she had done a little too much good in the morning; she held a grey veil drawn before her, the condensation of which was visibly being increased, and, as a result, the cypresses, which grew here and there in the Strada di Sepolcri, rose unusually sharp and black against the heavens. It was a picture different from that of yesterday; the brilliance which had mysteriously glittered over everything was lacking; the street also assumed a certain gloomy distinctness and had at present a dead aspect which honored its name. This impression was not diminished by an isolated movement at its end, but was rather heightened by it; there, in the vicinity of the Villa of Diomede, a phantom seemed to be looking for its grave, and disappeared under one of the monuments.

It was not the shortest way from the house of Meleager
to the "Albergo del Sole," rather the exactly opposite direction. But Zoë-Gradiva must have also decided that time was
not yet importuning so violently to lunch, for after a quite
brief stop at the gate of Hercules, she walked farther along
the lava-blocks of the Street of Tombs, every time raising
the sole of her lingering foot almost perpendicularly.

The Villa of Diomede—named thus, for people of the
present, after a monument which a certain freedman,
Marcus Arrius Diomedes, formerly promoted to the director-
ship of this city-section, had erected nearby for his lady,
Arria, as well as for himself and his relatives—was a very
extensive building and concealed within itself a part of the
history of the destruction of Pompeii not invented by imagination. A confusion of extensive ruins formed the upper part;
below lay an unusually large sunken garden surrounded by
a well-preserved portico of pillars with scanty remnants of
a fountain and a small temple in the middle; and farther
along two stairways led down to a circular cellar-vault,
lighted only dimly by gloomy twilight. The ashes of Vesuvius had penetrated into this also, and the skeletons of
eighteen women and children had been found here; seeking
protection, they had fled, with some hastily gathered provisions, into the half-subterranean space, and the deceptive
refuge had become the tomb of all. In another place the supposed, nameless master of the house lay, also stretched out
choked on the ground; he had wished to escape through the
locked garden door, for he held the key to it in his fingers.
Beside him cowered another skeleton, probably that of a
servant, who was carrying a considerable number of gold

and silver coins. The bodies of the unfortunates had been preserved by the hardened ashes; in the museum at Naples there is under glass the exact impression of the neck, shoulders, and beautiful bosom of a young girl clad in a fine, gauzy garment.

The Villa of Diomede had, at one time, at least, been the inevitable goal of every dutiful visitor to Pompeii; but now, at noon, in its rather roomy solitude, certainly no curiosity lingered in it, and therefore it had seemed to Norbert Hanold the place of refuge best suited to his newest mental needs. These longed most insistently for gravelike loneliness, breathless silence, and quiescent peace; against the latter, however, an impelling restlessness in his system raised counter-claims, and he had been obliged to force an agreement between the two demands, such that the mind tried to claim its own and yet gave the feet liberty to follow their impulse. So he had been wandering around through the portico since his entrance. He succeeded thus in preserving his bodily equilibrium, and he busied himself with changing his mental state into the same normal condition. That, however, seemed more difficult in execution than in intention. Of course it seemed to his judgment unquestionable that he had been utterly foolish and irrational to believe that he had sat with a young Pompeiian girl, who had become more or less corporeally alive again, and this clear view of his madness formed incontestably an essential advance on the return to sound reason. But it was not yet restored entirely to normal condition, for, even if it had occurred to him that Gradiva was only a dead bas-relief, it was also equally beyond doubt that she was still alive. For that irrefutable proof was adduced; not he alone, but others also, saw her, knew that her name was Zoë and spoke with her, as with a being as much alive, in substance, as they. On the other hand, however, she knew his name too, and again, that could originate only from a supernatural power; this dual nature remained enigmatic even for the rays of understanding that were entering his mind. Yet to this incompatible duality there was joined a similar one in him, for he cherished the earnest desire to have been destroyed here in the Villa of Diomede two thousand years ago, in order that he might not run the risk of meeting Zoë-Gradiva again anywhere; at the same time, however, an extraordinarily joyous feeling was stirring within him, because he was still alive and was therefore able to meet her again somewhere. To use a commonplace yet fitting simile, this was turning in his head like a millwheel, and through the long portico he ran around likewise without stopping, which did not aid him in the explanation of the contradictions. On the contrary, he was moved by an indefinite feeling that everything was growing darker and darker about and within him.

Then he suddenly recoiled, as he turned one of the four corners of the colonnade. A half-dozen paces away from him there sat, rather high up on a fragmentary wall-ruin, one of the young girls who had found death here in the ashes.

No, that was nonsense, which his reason rejected. His eyes, too, and a nameless something else recognized that fact. It was Gradiva; she was sitting on a stone ruin as she had formerly sat on the step; only, as the former was considerably higher, her slender feet, which hung down free in the sand-color shoes, were visible up to her dainty ankles.

With an instinctive movement, Norbert was at first about

to run out between the pillars through the garden. What, for a half-hour, he had feared most of anything in the world had suddenly appeared, viewed him with bright eyes and with lips which, he felt, were about to burst into mocking laughter. Yet they didn't, but the familiar voice rang out calmly from them, "You'll get wet outside."

Now, for the first time, he saw that it was raining; for that reason it had become so dark. That unquestionably was an advantage to all the plants about and in Pompeii, but that a human being in the place would be benefited by it was ridiculous, and for the moment Norbert Hanold feared, far more than danger of death, appearing ridiculous. Therefore he involuntarily gave up the attempt to get away, stood there, helpless, and looked at the two feet, which now, as if somewhat impatient, were swinging back and forth; and as this view did not have so clearing an effect upon his thoughts that he could find expression for them, the owner of the dainty feet again took up the conversation. "We were interrupted before; you were just going to tell me something about flies—I imagined that you were making scientific investigations here—or about a fly in your head. Did you succeed in catching and destroying the one on my hand?"

This last she said with a smiling expression about her lips, which, however, was so faint and charming that it was not at all terrifying. On the contrary, it now lent to the questioned man power of speech, but with the limitation that the young archaeologist suddenly did not know how to address her. In order to escape this dilemma, he found it best to avoid that and replied, "I was—as someone said—somewhat confused in my head and beg pardon that I—the hand—like that—how I could be so stupid I can't understand—but

I can't understand either how its owner could use my name in upbraiding me for my—my unreason."

Gradiva's feet stopped moving and she rejoined, still addressing him familiarly: "So your power of understanding has not yet progressed that far, Norbert Hanold. Of course, I cannot be surprised, for you have long ago accustomed me to it. To have that experience again, I need not have come to Pompeii, and you could have confirmed it for me a good hundred miles nearer."

"A hundred miles nearer," he repeated, perplexed and half stuttering; "where is that?"

"Diagonally across from your house, in the corner house; in my window there is a cage with a canary in it."

Like a memory from far away this last word moved the hearer, who repeated, "A canary." And he added, stuttering more, "He—he sings?"

"They usually do, especially in spring when the sun begins to seem warm again. In that house lives my father, Richard Bertgang, professor of Zoology."

Norbert Hanold's eyes opened to a width never before attained by them, and then he said, "Bertgang—then are you—are you Miss Zoë Bertgang? But she looked quite different—"

The two dangling feet began again to swing a little, and Miss Zoë Bertgang said in reply, "If you find that form of address* more suitable between us, I can use it, too, of course, but the other came to me more naturally. I don't know whether I looked different once, when we used to run about together as friends every day and occasionally beat and cuffed each other for a change; but if, in recent years,

* [See note, page 49 above.—Ed.]

you had favored me with even one glance, you might perhaps have noticed that I have looked like this for a long
time.—No, now, as they say, it's pouring pitchforks; you
won't have a dry stitch."

Not only had the feet of the speaker indicated a return
of impatience, or whatever it might be, but also in the tones
of her voice there appeared a little didactic, ill-humored
curtness, and Norbert had thereby been overwhelmed by a
feeling that he was running the risk of slipping into the role
of a big schoolboy scolded and slapped in the face. That
caused him to again seek mechanically for an exit between
the pillars, and to the movement which showed this impulse Miss Zoë's last utterance, indifferently added, had
reference; and, of course, in an undeniably striking way,
because, for what was now occurring outside of the shelter,
"pouring" was really a mild term. A tropical cloudburst, such
as only seldom took pity on the summer thirst of the
meadows of the Campagna, was shooting vertically and
rushing as if the Tyrrhenian Sea were pouring from heaven
upon the Villa of Diomede; and yet it continued like a firm
wall composed of billions of drops gleaming like pearls and
large as nuts. That, indeed, made escape out into the open
air impossible, and forced Norbert Hanold to remain in the
schoolroom of the portico while the young schoolmistress
with the delicate, clever face made use of the hindrance for
further extension of her pedagogical discussion by continuing, after a brief pause:

"In those days, up to the time when people, for some
unknown reason, call us 'Backfisch,' * I had really acquired a
strange attachment for you and thought that I could never

* [See note, page 52 above.—ED.]

find a more congenial friend in the world. I had no mother,
sister, or brother, you know; to my father, a slowworm in
alcohol was far more interesting than I, and people (I count
girls among them) must surely have something with which
they can occupy their thoughts and whatever else is connected with these. You were that something in those days.
But when archaeology had come over you, I made the discovery that you—excuse me for using the familiar form of
address, but your new formality sounds too absurd to me;
besides, it isn't suitable for what I want to express—as I was
saying, it turned out that you had become an unbearable
person who no longer had, at least for me, an eye in his
head, a tongue in his mouth, nor a memory in his head,
which is the place where I retain *my* memories of our childhood friendship. So I probably looked different from what
I did formerly, for when I occasionally met you at a party,
as recently as last winter, you did not look at me and I did
not hear your voice; in this, of course, there was nothing
that marked me out especially, for you treated all the others
in the same way. To you I was but air, and you, with your
shock of light hair, which I had once upon a time mussed up
so often, were as boring, shriveled-up, and tongue-tied as a
stuffed cockatoo and at the same time as grandiose as an—
*archaeopteryx;* I think that's the name of that excavated
antediluvian bird-monster. But that your head harbored an
imagination so magnificent as to consider me, here in Pompeii, as something excavated and restored to life—that I
had not surmised of you. And when you suddenly stood before me unexpectedly, it cost me some effort at first to understand what kind of incredible fantasy your imagination
had invented. Then I was amused and, in spite of its mad-

ness, it was not entirely displeasing to me. For, as I said, I had not expected it of you."

With that, her expression and tone somewhat mollified at the end, Miss Zoë Bertgang finished her unreserved, detailed, and instructive lecture. And it was indeed notable how exactly she then resembled the figure of Gradiva on the bas-relief, not only in her features, her form, her eyes, expressive of wisdom, and her charmingly wavy hair, but also in her graceful manner of walking which he had often seen. Her drapery, too—dress and scarf of a cream-colored, fine cashmere material which fell in soft, voluminous folds— completed the extraordinary resemblance of her whole appearance. There might have been much foolishness in the belief that a young Pompeiian girl, destroyed two thousand years ago by Vesuvius, could sometimes walk around alive again, speak, draw, and eat bread. But even if the belief brought happiness, a considerable amount of incomprehensibility had to be put up with; and in consideration of all the circumstances, there was incontestably present, in the judgment of Norbert Hanold, some mitigating ground for his madness in for two days considering Gradiva a resurrection.

Although he stood there dry under the portico roof, there was established, not quite ineptly, a comparison between him and a wet poodle, who has had a bucketful of water thrown on his head; but the cold shower had really done him good. Without knowing exactly why, he felt that he was breathing much more easily. In that, of course, the change of tone at the end of the sermon—for the speaker sat as if in a pulpit-chair—might have helped especially. At least thereat a transfigured light appeared in his eyes, such as awakened hope for salvation through faith produces in the eyes of an ardently affected churchgoer; and as the rebuke was now over, and there seemed no necessity for fearing a further continuation, he succeeded in saying, "Yes, now I recognize—no, you have not changed at all—it is you, Zoë —my good, happy, clever comrade—it is most strange—"

"To think that a person must first die to become alive; but for archaeologists that is necessary, I suppose."

"No, I mean your name—"

"Why is it strange?"

The young archaeologist showed himself familiar not only with the classical languages, but also with the etymology of German, and continued, "Because *Bertgang* has the same meaning as *Gradiva* and signifies 'the one splendid in walking.' "

Miss Zoë Bertgang's two sandal-like shoes were, for the moment, because of their movement, reminiscent of an impatiently seesawing wagtail waiting for something. Yet the possessor of the feet that walked so magnificently seemed not at present to be paying any attention to philological explanations. By her countenance she gave the impression of being occupied with some hasty plan, but was restrained from it by an exclamation of Norbert Hanold's which audibly emanated from deepest conviction, "What luck, though, that you are not Gradiva, but are like the congenial young lady!"

That caused an expression as of interested surprise to pass over her face and she asked, "Who is that? Whom do you mean?"

"The one who spoke to you in the house of Meleager."

"Do you know her?"

"Yes, I had already seen her. She was the first person who seemed especially congenial to me."

"So? Where did you see her?"

"This morning, in the House of the Faun. There the couple were doing something very strange."

"What were they doing?"

"They did not see me and they kissed each other.'

"That was really very sensible, you know. Why else are they in Pompeii on their wedding trip?"

At one blow with the last word the former picture changed before Norbert Hanold's eyes, for the old wall-ruin lay there empty, because the girl, who had chosen it as a seat, teacher's chair, and pulpit, had come down, or really flown, and with the same supple buoyancy as that of a wagtail swinging through the air, so that she already stood again on Gradiva-feet, before his glance had consciously caught up with her descent. And, continuing her speech directly, she said, "Well, the rain has stopped; too severe rulers do not reign long. That is sensible, too, you know, and thus everything has again become sensible. I, not least of all, and you can look up Gisa Hartleben, or whatever new name she has, to be of scientific assistance to her about the purpose of her stay in Pompeii. I must now go to the 'Albergo del Sole,' for my father is probably waiting for me already at lunch. Perhaps we shall meet again sometime at a party in Germany or on the moon. *Addio!*"

Zoë Bertgang said this in the absolutely polite, but also equally indifferent, tone of a most well-bred young lady, and, as was her custom, placing her left foot forward, raised the sole of the right almost perpendicularly to go out. As

she lifted her dress slightly with her left hand, because of
the thoroughly wet ground outside, the resemblance to
Gradiva was perfect, and the man, standing hardly more
than two arm-lengths away, noticed for the first time a quite
insignificant deviation in the living picture from the stone
one. The latter lacked something possessed by the former,
which appeared at the moment quite clear—a little dimple
in her cheek, which produced a slight, indefinable effect. It
puckered and wrinkled a little and could therefore express
annoyance or a suppressed impulse to laugh, possibly both
together. Norbert Hanold looked at it, and although from
the evidence just presented to him he had completely regained his reason, his eyes had to again submit to an optical
illusion. For, in a tone triumphing peculiarly over his discovery, he cried out, "There is the fly again!"

It sounded so strange that from the uncomprehending listener, who could not see herself, escaped the question, "The
fly—where?"

"There on your cheek!" and immediately the man, as he
answered, suddenly twined an arm about her neck and
snapped, this time with his lips, at the insect so deeply
abhorrent to him, which vision juggled before his eyes deceptively in the little dimple. Apparently, however, without success, for right afterwards he cried again, "No, now
it's on your lips!" And thereupon, quick as a flash, he directed thither his attempt to capture, now remaining so long
that no doubt could survive that he succeeded in completely
accomplishing his purpose. Strange to relate, the living
Gradiva did not hinder him at all; and when her mouth,
after about a minute, was forced to struggle for breath,
restored to powers of speech, she did not say, "You are ob-

viously crazy, Norbert Hanold," but rather allowed a most charming smile to play more visibly than before about her red lips. She had been convinced more than ever of the complete recovery of his reason.

The Villa of Diomede had two thousand years ago seen and heard horrible things in an evil hour; yet at the present it heard and saw, for about an hour, only things not at all suited to inspire horror. Then, however, a sensible idea became uppermost in Miss Zoë Bertgang's mind and as a result, she said, against her wishes, "Now, I must *really* go, or my poor father will starve. It seems to me you can today forgo Gisa Hartleben's company at noon, for you have nothing more to learn from her and ought to be content with us in the Sun Hotel."

From this it was to be concluded that during that hour something must have been discussed, for it indicated a helpful desire to instruct, which the young lady vented on Norbert. Yet, from the reminding words, he did not gather this, but something which, for the first time, he was becoming terribly conscious of. This was apparent in the repetition, "Your father—what will he—?"

Miss Zoë, however, interrupted, without any sign of awakened anxiety, "Probably he will do nothing; I am not an indispensable piece in his zoological collection; if I were, my heart would perhaps not have clung to you so unwisely. Besides, from my early years, I have been sure that a woman is of use in the world only when she relieves a man of the trouble of deciding household matters; I generally do this for my father and therefore you can also be rather at ease about your future. Should he, however, by chance, in this case have an opinion different from mine, we will make it as simple as possible. You go over to Capri for a couple of days; there, with a grass snare—you can practice making them on my little finger—catch a lizard *faraglionensis*. Let it go here again, and catch it before his eyes. Then give him free choice between it and me, and you will have me so surely that I am sorry for you. Toward his colleague, Eimer, however, I feel today that I have formerly been ungrateful, for without his genial invention of lizard-catching I should probably not have come into the house of Meleager, and that would have been a shame, not only for you, but for me too."

This last view she expressed outside of the Villa of Diomede; and, alas, there was no person present on earth who could make any statements about the voice and manner of talking of Gradiva. Yet even if they had resembled those of Zoë Bertgang, as everything else about her did, they must have possessed a quite unusually beautiful and roguish charm.

By this, at least, Norbert Hanold was so strongly overwhelmed that, exalted to poetic flights, he cried out, "Zoë, you dear life and lovely present—we shall take our wedding trip to Italy and Pompeii."

That was a decided proof of how different circumstances can also produce a transformation in a human being and at the same time unite with it a weakening of the memory. For it did not occur to him at all that he would thereby expose himself and his companion on the journey to the danger of receiving, from misanthropic, ill-humored railway companions, the names Augustus and Gretchen. But at the moment he was thinking so little about it that they walked along hand in hand through the old Street of Tombs in Pompeii.

Of course this, too, did not stamp itself into their minds at present as such, for a cloudless sky shone and laughed again above it; the sun stretched out a golden carpet on the old lava-blocks; Vesuvius spread its misty pine-cone; and the whole excavated city seemed overwhelmed, not with pumice and ashes, but with pearls and diamonds, by the beneficent rainstorm.

The brilliance in the eyes of the young daughter of the zoologist rivaled these. But to the announced desire about the destination of their journey by her childhood friend who had, in a way, also been excavated from the ashes, her wise lips responded: "I think we won't worry about that today; that is a thing which may better be left by both of us to more and maturer consideration and future promptings. I, at least, do not yet feel quite alive enough now for such geographical decisions."

That showed that the speaker possessed great modesty about the quality of her insight into things about which she had never thought until today. They had arrived again at the gate of Hercules, where, at the beginning of the Strada Consolare, old steppingstones crossed the street. Norbert Hanold stopped before them and said with a peculiar tone, "Please go ahead here." A merry, comprehending, laughing expression lurked around his companion's mouth, and, raising her dress slightly with her left hand, Gradiva *rediviva* Zoë Bertgang, viewed by him with dreamily observing eyes, crossed with her calmly buoyant walk, through the sunlight, over the steppingstones, to the other side of the street.

# Index

Ambiguity, 108-111
Ambition, 126
Andreas-Salome, Lou, 12
Anxiety-dream: and rejection of unconscious wish, 118; as libidinous emotion, 84; example in Hanold, 83
Art: as emotive statement, 13; as public companion to dream, 9; as way into depths, 10; exploitation by Jungians, 10; Freud's treatment of, 10-11, 15-16; latent in everyone, 10; made less necessary by science, 12; "manifest" and "latent" content of, 16

Bleuler, E., 76 n
Breuer, Josef, 77, 77 n, 113
Brill, A. A., 76 n, 77 n

"Cathartic" treatment of delusion, 113-114
Chance in human life, 63
Charcot, Jean Martin, 76
Cobbe, Frances Power, 9 n
Comte, Auguste, 4
"Condensation," 15, 99-100

Daydreaming: and poet, 129-133; as play substitute, 124-125, 132; characteristics of, 126-127; child's play distinguished from, 123
Degenerate, 66-67
Delusion: absurdities in chronic cases of, 94-95; accompanied by degree of truth, 104; and control by fantasies, 66; "cathartic" treatment of, 113-114; destruction by acceptance, 41-42, 92-93; disposition for formation of, 68; expressed by psychic symptoms, 66; rooted in repression, 86; symptoms of, as result of compromise, 74
De Sanctis, Sante, 78 n
"Displacement," 15; distortion by, 81
Dream: ambiguity of, 16, 111; and fairy tales, 135-142; as myth, 9 n; as wish-fulfillment, 25, 117-118; connected with mental disturbance, 78; influenced by recent activities, 80, 97, 100-101, 118, 137; lacks power to communicate, 9-10; not prevision of future, 25; of castration, 142; relation to fantasy, 128; rooted in repression, 85-86; scientific evaluation of, 26; use of by creative writers, 26-28
Dream interpretation: associations of patient needed for, 2, 62, 86; customary limitations, 78-79; method, 82, 96-98; "over-interpretation" necessary for, 16; psychoanalytic, 2; symbolic, 2

Ego, 12, 20, 130-131
Emerson, Ralph Waldo, 9
"Endopsychic" perception, 73
Eroticism: as root of fetishism, 68; incomplete in childhood, 68; leads to fantasies, 126; rejection of, example, 90-91; restoration of respect for, 112

236